Your One-Stop
Guide to
the Bible

Your One-Stop Guide to the Bible

KEVIN PERROTTA

CHARIS

SERVANT PUBLICATIONS
ANN ARBOR, MICHIGAN

Charis Books is an imprint of Servant Publications especially designed to
serve Roman Catholics.

NIHIL OBSTAT: Monsignor Robert D. Lunsford
                Chancellor
IMPRIMATUR: Most Reverend Carl F. Mengeling
                Bishop of Lansing
                August 10, 2000

The NIHIL OBSTAT and IMPRIMATUR are a declaration that a book
or pamphlet is considered to be free from doctrinal or moral error. It is
not implied that those who have granted the NIHIL OBSTAT and
IMPRIMATUR agree with the contents, opinions, or statements expressed.

Servant Publications
P.O. Box 8617
Ann Arbor, MI 48107

Cover design by Hile Illustration and Design, Ann Arbor, Michigan

00 01 02 03 10 9 8 7 6 5 4 3 2 1

Printed in the United States of America
ISBN 1-56955-208-8

LIBRARY OF CONGRESS CATALOGING-IN-PUBLICATION DATA

Perotta, Kevin
     Your one-stop guide to the Bible / by Kevin Perotta.
         p. cm.
     Includes bibliographical references and index.
     ISBN 1-56955-208-8 (alk. paper)
     1. Bible–Introductions. 2. Catholic Church–Doctrines. I. Title.

BS475.2 .P46 2001
220.6'1–dc21   00-064363

Contents

Preface

If you know anything at all about the Bible, you know that a complete one-stop guide to the Bible is no more possible than a postcard of the human genome. The Bible is just a *little* too big and too deep for a single book to supply all the help a reader needs. What *is* possible is a *first-stop* guide to the Bible—a book that gives you a basic orientation to what the Bible is, how to make sense of it, and how to read it as God's word to you. That is the purpose of this book.

There is no way to talk about the Bible without introducing a few names and dates, facts and figures, technical terms, and even a word or two of Hebrew and Greek. But at the beginning of your discovery of the Bible, it is more important to get the big picture than to absorb a lot of data. So I have kept the details to a minimum. A good study Bible, that is, an edition of the Bible with explanatory articles and plentiful notes, will provide you with a wealth of details. The present book will help you see why you would want to know all those details. (Chapter nine provides information on selecting a study Bible.)

The Bible is simple and complex. Because it is simple, you can start reading it without special preparation. Yet as soon as you begin to read, you meet questions not easily answered. Consequently an introductory book must deal with some difficult subjects. I have tried to begin every chapter at an elementary level, but a few of them have a steep learning curve. If you find a chapter heavy going (I'm thinking particularly of chapter seven on interpretation) you might skim it and return to it later on.

Again, if you know anything about the study of the Bible, you know that there are scholarly debates about virtually every aspect of it. Before many statements in this book, I could have put the qualification, "in the view of many scholars...." After many statements I could have written, "...although some scholars reach different conclusions." Rather than cluttering up the book that way, it seemed simpler just to say here that I have necessarily had to make choices between various scholarly opinions. Not everyone with expertise about the Bible would agree with every statement I make. Throughout the book, however, I have followed the findings and conclusions of mainstream biblical scholars. And I have consistently tried to be in harmony with Catholic teaching.

I have not used footnotes. But you will find bibliographic information about the works quoted throughout the book in chapter ten on resources.

Well now, onward into the Bible, guided in our exploration by the words of St. Augustine: "Let them pray, so that they might understand."

Chapter One

What Have We Here?
The Bible at First Glance

When you pick up a Bible, you hold more than a book. You have a library in your hands. The word *Bible* comes from the Greek language. In ancient Greek, *biblion* meant a book written on a scroll; the plural, *ta biblia,* meant the books, or a library.

It is fitting that this library should have a Greek name, for a good deal of it was written in Greek. An even larger portion was written in Hebrew. A few sections were written in a sister-language to Hebrew called Aramaic. So what most of us hold in our hands is a translation—a point we will consider in chapter nine.

The Bible is less like the public library down the street and more like the collection of books in your house. The books in my house reflect the tastes and background of our family. The Bible reflects the history, needs, and interests of the people of God. Why they chose these books while excluding similar works is a point we will consider in chapter six.

Every library has some kind of order to it. As we will see in the next chapter, the Bible has a rather careful arrangement. Unlike most library collections, it has a beginning and an end: thus it is a book, as well as a collection of books.

The Bible has two main parts. The first, longer part, begins with accounts of the creation of the world and then focuses on the fortunes of a small, ancient Near Eastern people called Israel—a people who continue in the modern world as the Jewish people. The first part traces their ups and downs over more than a thousand years, ending about a century before Jesus. The second part begins by recounting Jesus' life, death, and resurrection. It continues with a narrative about his followers and then a collection of early Christian letters. It concludes with a symbolic vision of history, the end of the world, and a new creation.

The Bible, Catholics, and Jews

The collection of books that Catholics call the Old Testament overlaps with the collection that constitutes the Bible for Jews (see boxes on pages 14, 26, and 74 for differences between the biblical collections of Jews, Catholics, and Protestants). When speaking with Jews, what can Catholics call these books they have in common with them?

Simply calling these books "Scripture" is appropriate. Catholics should be aware that Jews do not use the term "Old Testament," since for them these books are not a prelude to a further testament but are simply the Bible. Furthermore, many Jews find Christians' use of the term "Old Testament" offensive, because old seems to imply that God's covenant with Israel has been abolished and replaced by a covenant through Jesus. The Catholic Church does not, in fact, believe that the covenant between God and Israel has come to an end. Thus, it is best for Catholics not to use the term "Old Testament" in conversations with Jews.

An increasingly popular substitute for Old Testament is the term "Hebrew Scriptures" (with a corresponding term—"Christian Scriptures"—for the New Testament).

This approach avoids giving any offense to Jews. A drawback, however, is that it may seem to imply that the first portion of the Bible belongs only to Judaism and not to Christianity also.

An alternative for Christians in their conversations with Jews is to use the terms "First Testament" and "Second Testament" or the less formal terminology that Pope John Paul II used when he spoke with Jewish leaders in Mainz, Germany, in December 1980—"the first and the second parts of the Bible."

Within the Church, it remains appropriate for Christians to continue to speak of Old and New Testaments. In 1999, the American bishops affirmed that these terms are part of the "language of faith" and should continue to be used in Catholic materials for religious education.

In Christian tradition the two parts have been called "testaments." In this usage, the term "testament" refers to a covenant—a solemn agreement binding two parties together, as in marriage. "Testament" is used because each of the Bible's two main parts is organized around a covenant. The first part, which in Christian tradition is called the Old Testament, revolves around the covenant God made with the people Israel through their leader Moses. The second part, called the New Testament, focuses on the covenant God has made with the entire human race through Jesus Christ. The "testament" terminology indicates the Bible's main subject: the faithful, covenant relationship that God wishes to have with us, his human creatures.

As any library, the Bible contains books written by many authors—and shaped by many editors. While it testifies to historical events, not all of it is history. Among its books are a collection of prayers (Psalms), reflections on life (Proverbs and other "wisdom" books), social analysis and predictions of God's actions (prophetic books), and personal letters (for example, Philemon). There is even a small shelf of fiction containing short stories, one of which is pretty funny (Jonah).

Chapter Two

What's the Message?
The Bible's Big Picture

If the Bible is a library of ancient books, why read it? There are lots of ancient texts lying around in museums—pressed onto clay tablets or scratched onto sheets of papyrus. We leave most of them to specialists. What is so different about the biblical books that we should read them, even if we are not terribly interested in ancient history and literature? The answer lies in the Bible's message, a message that is as fresh and important today as it was two thousand years ago.

To grasp the Bible's message, a good place to begin is the table of contents. The Bible tells a story. The way the books are shelved in the biblical library points us toward the story line and thus toward the central message.

We have already seen that the Bible is divided into two parts—the Old and New Testaments. If you look closely, you will notice that within each part the books are grouped according to types.

The Books of the Catholic Bible

OLD TESTAMENT

Historical Books
The Pentateuch

Genesis	Numbers
Exodus	Deuteronomy
Leviticus	

Other historical works

Joshua	Ezra
Judges	Nehemiah
Ruth	Tobit
1 and 2 Samuel	Judith
1 and 2 Kings	Esther
1 and 2 Chronicles	1 and 2 Maccabees

Reflective or Prayerful Books

Job	Song of Songs
Psalms	Wisdom
Proverbs	Sirach
Ecclesiastes	

Prophetic Books
The major prophets

Isaiah	Baruch
Jeremiah	Ezekiel
Lamentations	Daniel

The minor prophets

Hosea	Nahum
Joel	Habakkuk
Amos	Zephaniah
Obadiah	Haggai
Jonah	Zechariah
Micah	Malachi

NEW TESTAMENT

Narratives
Gospels
Matthew
Mark
Luke
John

Narrative about the early Church
Acts of the Apostles

Correspondence
Letters associated with Paul
Romans
1 and 2 Corinthians
Galatians
Ephesians
Philippians
Colossians
1 and 2 Thessalonians
1 and 2 Timothy
Titus
Philemon
Hebrews

Letters associated with other figures
James
1 and 2 Peter
1, 2, and 3 John
Jude

A Vision
Revelation

Note: Some of the Old Testament books recognized by the Catholic Church are not recognized by Protestants and are not part of the Bible recognized by Judaism. These are Tobit, Judith, 1 and 2 Maccabees, Wisdom, Sirach, Baruch, and parts of Daniel and Esther. Catholics call these the "deuterocanonical" (that is, "second" portion) works; others refer to them as the "apocrypha" (literally "hidden" works, here meaning inauthentic). See pages 74-76.

The Old Testament

The first grouping consists mainly of *Historical Books.* The placement of historical books at the beginning of the Bible tells us something right away: the Bible speaks about history. It is concerned with the real world, not some religious-greeting-card, never-never land. True, the Bible contains poems, visions, legends, even some worked-over mythical material. Biblical authors employ symbolic language to speak about God (God led the Israelites out of Egypt "by a mighty hand and an outstretched arm"—Deuteronomy 4:34) because there is no way to avoid metaphors and analogies when speaking of him. Nevertheless, the Bible is historical in its guts and bones. It testifies to God's activity in our twenty-four-hours-a-day-seven-days-a-week world.

To be precise, however, the historical section of the Bible leads off with some chapters that are not really history (and regarding Ruth, Tobit, Judith, and Esther see page 52). The first eleven chapters of the first book, Genesis ("origin"), recount God's creation of the world and prehistoric events—Adam and Eve, Cain and Abel, Noah and the flood, the tower of Babel, and so on. This unit is prehistory rather than history. It shows that God created the earth as home for a race of creatures with whom he wishes to have a deep, lasting relationship—the human race (see Genesis 1–2). It also identifies the root of human unhappiness: we humans have not wholeheartedly embraced God's purposes. By turning away from God, we have brought conflict, suffering, even death, on ourselves (see Genesis 3–11).

The historical books show that God did not give up on us but put into effect a plan for restoring us to himself. In pursuit of this plan, God gathered and spoke to the people called Israel. In this people, God began to restore the wholeness, peace, and closeness to him that he had wished the human race to enjoy from the beginning.

After chapter eleven, Genesis tells of God's call to Israel's semi-nomadic ancestors (Abraham, Sarah, and others) and his promises to them of protection, offspring, and land (see Genesis 12–50). The next book, Exodus ("going out"), tells of his bringing their descendants out of slavery in Egypt around the year 1250 B.C. and making a covenant with them in the desert of Sinai (see Exodus 1–18). God instructs them in the way he wishes them to live (see Exodus 19–40, Leviticus, Numbers). Then, through Moses, God urges them to be faithful to his instructions (Deuteronomy). Thus the first five books, called the Pentateuch, establish the basis for God's dealings with Israel as a people.

At the end of the Pentateuch, the reader wonders how the Israelites will respond. A sequence of historical books provides the answer:

B.C. and A.D.

"B.C." stands for "Before Christ," "A.D." for "Anno Domini," Latin for "In the Year of the Lord." Both designations are traditional in Western culture and, according to the American Catholic bishops, are part of the "language of faith" and should continue to be used in religious education. In other settings, a common alternative is "B.C.E." and "C.E.," meaning "Before Common Era" and "Common Era."

- The Israelites enter the land of Canaan (roughly modern Israel and Palestinian territories), around 1200 B.C. (the book of Joshua).
- They experience a period of tribal confederation— roughly 1200 to 1020 B.C. (the book of Judges).
- They enjoy a brief national "moment in the sun" as a powerful kingdom under kings David and Solomon, from 1000 to 922 B.C. (1 and 2 Samuel; 1 Kings 1–11; 1 Chronicles 11–2 Chronicles 9).
- They endure the break-up of the nation into northern and southern kingdoms (called respectively "Israel" and "Judah"), decline and military defeat, and the deportation of leading members of the southern kingdom to Babylon—in present-day Iraq—in 587 B.C. (the rest of the books of Kings and Chronicles).

These historical books underline God's desire for Israel to be fully devoted to him and to stay clear of their neighbors' worship of many gods with their militarism, economic oppression, and sexual immorality. God's longing for the Israelites to be faithful to him and to show justice and kindness toward one another meets with a generally disappointing response. The Israelites show a deep-seated inclination to worship other gods, to mistreat each other, to ignore God's warnings, and to turn to God only in crisis. Thus they exemplify the spiritual and moral flaws that all human beings share. God shows himself to be patient, yet unwilling to allow infidelity and injustice to go unchecked indefinitely. Finally, he allows the Israelites to be overwhelmed by their enemies.

As Jerusalem burns and the Israelites are dragged off into captivity at the end of 2 Kings, the story of God and Israel launched in the Pentateuch seems to have ended in failure. But some fifty years later, God opens the way for some exiles to return from Babylon to Jerusalem. They go home with a determination not to repeat the former mistakes. Thus the sequence of historical writings resumes and we see:

- The return of exiles from Babylon; their restoration of the Jerusalem temple and a small-scale community life beginning about 539 B.C. (the books of Ezra and Nehemiah).
- Their struggles against Greek-speaking emperors in Syria beginning around 175 B.C. (the books of the Maccabees).

Scrolls

The biblical books were originally written on papyrus scrolls rather than on pages bound between covers. The practice of writing on scrolls is reflected in the name sometimes given to the first five books of the Bible, Pentateuch, which is Greek for "five cases for holding scrolls." Beyond a certain length, a scroll became unwieldy. Books beyond that limit would be divided between two scrolls. Three of the historical books were long enough to require two scrolls each. Thus we have 1 and 2 Samuel, 1 and 2 Kings, and 1 and 2 Chronicles (1 and 2 Maccabees are separate histories). Their separation into two parts in the days of scroll-writing has carried over into today's published Bibles, even though the division is no longer necessary.

From the historical books a portrait of God emerges: he is forgiving, generous, loyal, deeply concerned about justice among people, reluctant to discipline yet insistent on people responding to his love. Because God is consistently merciful and faithful, patterns of rescue and blessing emerge in his dealings with Israel. His earlier actions become models (in discussions of the Bible sometimes called "types") of later actions. For example, God's leading his people out of slavery in Egypt (see Exodus 14) sets the pattern for his later leading them out of Babylon (see Isaiah 43:14-21).

At the conclusion of the historical books, Israel has not found lasting peace and wholeness. Yet God's actions recounted in these books give grounds for confidence that he has something further in mind. The God of such a good creation, the merciful God of the exodus, the God of covenant faithfulness toward Israel in exile—how could *this* God settle for anything less than his people's complete freedom from every source of evil? By revealing a God whose compassion and loyalty extends across centuries, the historical books stand not only as a record of God's past actions but as witness to a God who will surely act in the future.

The next Old Testament grouping consists of ***Reflective or Prayerful Books.*** These books do not chart the forward movement of God's plans but rather the deepening of his people's minds and hearts. Here we find personal prayers and community hymns (Psalms), folk wisdom (Proverbs), discussions of individual and social life (Job, Ecclesiastes, Wisdom, Sirach), even love poetry (the Song of Songs). The people of Israel ponder God's covenant and the way of life he has given them and speak to him in appeals, complaints, thanksgiving, and praise.

The final Old Testament grouping—*Prophetic Books*— resumes the focus on God's engagement with history. These books preserve the messages of men whom God authorized to speak for him in the period covered by the historical books. The grouping is only broadly prophetic because one work of historical fiction (about the real-life prophet Jonah) has found its way into this group, and a couple of nonprophetic books (Lamentations and Baruch) are shelved here because of their traditional association with the prophet Jeremiah.

The prophets did not speak general truths into a social vacuum. They presented God's penetrating analysis of actual people and institutions. By the prophets' words, God communicated his view of how well his people were conducting their political, cultural, and religious life. Through the prophets, God injected his judgment-bringing and life-sustaining words into historical situations (see Jeremiah 23:29; compare 1 Kings 17:1, 7.

For the most part, the prophets communicated God's purposes for their own present and near future, without envisaging distant ages to come. But their prophecies were not exhausted in their own times, because the divine promises they conveyed were not entirely fulfilled. The return from Babylon fell short of the predicted glory, receiving only token fulfillment (compare the grand predictions of Isaiah 60–62 and Ezekiel 36:22-38; 40:1–43:12 with the modest fulfillment in Ezra 3–4, Nehemiah 1–5; and Haggai 1). The prophets looked forward to God's acting on a global, even cosmic scale, and acting at a profound depth within men and women. They promised that God would reconcile his people to himself (see Isaiah 44:21-23), heal them of their tendency to resist him (see Jeremiah 31:31-34), renew the earth (see Isaiah 55:12-13;

65:17-25), remove injustice (see Isaiah 59:15-20), gather his scattered people (see Isaiah 49:8-21; Zechariah 10:6-12), overcome their enemies (see Isaiah 41:11-16; 49:22-26), and dwell splendidly in their midst (see Isaiah 52:7-12; 54:4-8). In sum, God would achieve his original intentions for humankind. These promises hung in the air, awaiting a humanly incomprehensible fulfillment.

Thus there is a surplus of expectation in the prophets' words, carried forward to a later time. The prophetic books, even more than the historical books, give rise to the expectation that God has great things in store for Israel and the world. The Church brings out this forward thrust by placing the prophetic books at the end of the Old Testament. The Old Testament concludes on a note of expectancy (see Malachi 4), peering into the future to see what God will yet do.

The New Testament

As the Old Testament begins with a historical section, so also the New. Although Jesus announced the coming of a divine kingdom not *of* this world (see John 18:36), he and the New Testament writers, like the figures of the Old Testament, were intensely concerned with events *in* this world.

Among the *Narratives* of the New Testament, the Gospels ("announcements of good news") hold pride of place. They report on Jesus' life, death, and resurrection. The Gospels' position immediately after the Old Testament signals that they announce the fulfillment of the expectations that God aroused in Israel through his saving actions and prophetic words. Indeed, in the Gospels God attains the purpose he had pursued since his creation of the human race. God's revelation of himself in the human world achieves perfection with his actual entry into this world through the birth of his Son as a human individual, Jesus of Nazareth. All of God's previous words reach their culmination in the taking-flesh of the divine Word (see John 1:1-14). The patterns, or types, of God's merciful dealings with Israel reach their fullest expression in Jesus and the life he brings. In him, God accomplishes the decisive exodus—from the slavery of sin and death into freedom and eternal life. God's activity to save human beings from evil comes to a climax in Jesus, who overcomes the fateful alienation between God and the human race that arose at the start of human existence (see Genesis 3). Through Jesus, God grants men and women an infinitely deep covenant with himself, a covenant by which the Spirit of God comes to live in human hearts.

Jesus claimed to enjoy an utterly unique relationship with God and to stand at the apex of God's dealings with Israel (see John 5:19-47). With his own appearance on the scene, Jesus announced, the arrival of God's kingdom had become imminent (see Mark 1:14-15). Jesus pointed to himself as the one who would fulfill God's promises to free Israel from her enemies, to gather his people, to grant them forgiveness and restoration, to establish God's more glorious presence among them.

But Jesus' fulfillment of Israel's God-given expectations was radically unexpected. He set himself to defeat not the Roman occupiers but the powers of human sinfulness, the devil, death itself. He conquered these powers not by military might but by self-sacrificing love, allowing himself to be nailed to a cross. He restored God's people not by a more exact observance of the details of the Mosaic law or through an enhancement of the

Jerusalem temple but by gathering disciples, laying down his life for them, and giving them the Holy Spirit. Jesus' renewal of Israel, then, was not a Jewish national renewal in the ancestral homeland but a universal renewal into which all men and women were to be invited. In this way, Jesus fulfilled the global purposes for which God had chosen and formed Israel.

By grouping the Gospels together at the beginning of the New Testament, the Church expresses the priority of Jesus. This point emerges clearly from the placement of the Gospel of Luke and the Acts of the Apostles. These two books were written by Luke as a two-volume work. Yet the two are separated so that Luke's Gospel might stand with the other three Gospels in lead position. The Gospels first! Jesus first!

With the Gospels, the forward thrust of God's actions and promises reaches its goal. The arrow hits the target. Yet the Gospels, too, point forward. God's action through Jesus now extends outward to embrace men and women everywhere until the end of history. Each Gospel ends with Jesus' assurance of his continued presence with his followers as they go out to offer all men and women—us!—the invitation to join his community and experience life in his Spirit.

Jesus has fulfilled the purposes of God in a way that is definitive but not yet fully manifest. Forgiveness, the gift of the Spirit, empowerment for personal and social transformation— these aspects of God's kingdom are now present. But there remains a more comprehensive coming of the kingdom, when God will cleanse creation of evil and unite men and women with himself forever, new creatures in a new creation. Jesus' resurrection is the beginning of this new creation; its completion is yet to come.

The Gospels, then, are not the end of the Bible, but its

watershed. The Old Testament books tracked God's actions leading up to Jesus' coming. The remainder of the New Testament books enlarge on the meaning and implications of his coming.

Shelved immediately after the Gospels is the Acts of the Apostles—volume two of Luke's narrative work. In this history of the beginnings of the Church, Luke shows how the news of Jesus began to spread throughout the world. Acts breaks off without a neat conclusion—deliberately, it seems. By its incompleteness, the ending looks toward the future—toward us, who are invited to enter into this unfinished history and help to complete it.

Correspondence. Just as the narrative books of the Old Testament are followed by reflections and prayers, the narrative books of the New Testament are followed by reflections (with prayers) on who Jesus is, what he has accomplished, and how we should respond to him. The content is not academic theology. These are letters from Christian leaders—Paul, James, Peter, John, Jude, and perhaps some of their followers—to communities of Christians struggling to understand Jesus and follow him in their particular circumstances. The letters were down-to-earth messages about the life and mission of Christ's first-century followers—messages that continue to speak to us in our real-world situations. A forward-looking orientation runs throughout the letters. From beginning to end, this early Christian correspondence is marked by the expectation of Jesus' glorious return to complete the coming of God's kingdom.

A Vision. The Old Testament ends with a group of prophetic works, the New Testament with a single prophetic work—the book of Revelation (or the "Apocalypse"—Greek for "an unveiling" or "a revealing"). This visionary work is the climax of prophecy, for in symbolic language it portrays Jesus' death and resurrection as the climax of God's action in the world and shows the impact of that event on the period of history between Jesus' resurrection and his return. This final New Testament book, and thus the Bible as a whole, concludes with its gaze directed toward the future, awaiting God's fulfillment of his plans for the human race. Thus the arrangement of the biblical books expresses the course of God's interactions with the human race from creation to new creation.

The ordering of the biblical books displays the working out of a single, overarching, divine plan—a plan to give life to the human race, a plan that expresses God's faithful, patient love. We who read the Bible in the twenty-first century find ourselves drawn into the final stage of God's activity in history (we cannot know how long it will last). We are called to prepare for the fulfillment of his plans, when he will bring to perfection his reign over all that he has created.

The Jewish Bible

TORAH ("INSTRUCTION," OR "LAW")

Genesis
Exodus
Leviticus
Numbers
Deuteronomy

NEVI'IM ("PROPHETS")

The Former Prophets

Joshua	1 and 2 Samuel
Judges	1 and 2 Kings

The Latter Prophets
The Twelve

Isaiah	Hosea	Nahum
Jeremiah	Joel	Habakkuk
Ezekiel	Amos	Zephaniah
	Obadiah	Haggai
	Jonah	Zechariah
	Micah	Malachi

KETUVIM ("WRITINGS")

Psalms	Ecclesiastes
Proverbs	Esther
Job	Daniel
Song of Songs	Ezra
Ruth	Nehemiah
Lamentations	1 and 2 Chronicles

The Jewish, or Hebrew, Bible is sometimes called Tanakh, an acronym for *T*orah, *N*evi'im, *K*etuvim. While overlapping with the Catholic Old Testament, the two collections differ in a couple of ways. (1) Tanakh is shorter than the Catholic Old Testament. Compare this listing of books with the Catholic Old Testament on page 14, and also see pages 74–76. (2) The books are arranged in a different order. In the Hebrew Bible, the first five books constitute a distinct section, called the Torah, meaning instruction, or law. Marked off as a unit, these five books form the foundation of Jewish belief and practice. The second section, called the Prophets, is different from the prophetic section of the Catholic Old Testament, since it includes four historical narratives (called the Former Prophets). The third section, the Writings, does not exactly correspond to the wisdom section of the Catholic Old Testament since it includes history and prophecy. The placement of Chronicles at the end of the Writings gives Tanakh a closure different from the future-oriented ending of the Catholic Old Testament created by placing the prophetic books in final position.

How Did It Come to Be?
The Formation of the Bible

The question, "How did it come to be?" probably does not spring to your mind whenever you pick up a book. Readers are usually less interested in the author's labors than in the result. Why should it be any different when it comes to the Bible? The reason is that the Bible developed very differently from modern books. Understanding the process is invaluable for understanding the outcome.

A modern book typically begins with someone who can read and write. An individual author or team of authors produces the manuscript in a fairly short period. Customarily the author writes in his or her own name. Although an editor makes suggestions and changes, the book emerges from the press as an expression of the author's views. There is a strong interest in presenting something new—new ideas, new information, new approach.

Sprinkle the words "not" and "not necessarily" throughout the preceding paragraph and you will begin to get an idea of how the Bible was produced. That is to say:

- Some of the material in the Bible originated with people who probably did not read or write (for example, the families of Abraham, Isaac, and Jacob). Some of it comes from literate people who preferred to express themselves orally (for example, Samuel and Jesus).

- Although some biblical books are the work of individual writers (the prophecy of Micah, Paul's letter to the Galatians), many reflect the efforts of multiple contributors (Exodus, Proverbs). The contributors did not all necessarily work as a team; they may have lived in different places, even in different centuries (Genesis, Isaiah).

- A succession of people added to and reshaped the texts, thus blurring the distinction between writing and editing (Deuteronomy, perhaps John). To a great extent the texts reflect the views of a community rather than of individual authors.

- More often than not it is impossible to determine who the writers and editors were (Chronicles, Hebrews) or even when they lived (Ruth, Psalms). Authors generally hid their identity because they were not seeking to promote their own views but to hand on traditions that conveyed God's revelation.

- The authors and editors enlarged or revised the oral and written traditions they received, so that the traditions might speak afresh to their own time. Nevertheless, they felt a serious obligation not to offer something new but to pass on faithfully what they had received (for this mentality, see Luke 1:1-4; 1 Corinthians 11:23-26; 15:1-7; 1 John 1:1-4).

Thus few, if any, of the books in the biblical library are books in the modern sense—writings composed in a person's own name, expressing his or her individual views. While many distinctive voices make themselves heard in the Bible, to some degree all the biblical books are the crystallizations of traditions handed on by many people. The Bible is the written form of the traditions of Israel and the early Church.

From Oral Traditions to Finished Product

The Bible's neat table of contents offers no hint of the long and sometimes untidy processes that led to the finished product. To bring this dimension of the biblical books into view, let us take a quick walk through the historical periods during which the biblical books were under construction. The point of the following survey is not to indicate exactly when and how each of the biblical books was composed (in most cases there are complicated scholarly debates over these matters), but to give a feel for the length and complexity of the development that the biblical books passed through on their way to their final form. The rounded dates are approximations.

Undetermined centuries before 1250 B.C. God spoke to the ancestors of Israel—Abraham, Sarah, and others—promising them the blessings of offspring and land. They wrote nothing. For unknown generations, their descendants handed on traditions about these patriarchs and matriarchs by word of mouth.

1250 to 1200 B.C.: Exodus from Egypt, covenant, desert years, entry into Canaan. The Israelites added recollections of these great events to their growing stock of community lore. They may have put down brief accounts or songs on papyrus, but for the most part they continued to pass on their traditions in spoken form.

1200 to 1000 B.C.: The period of tribal settlement. Tales of God's action through leaders such as Deborah and Samson were added to the community's oral traditions. A few of God's instructions for his people's way of life were put in writing by the prophet Samuel (see 1 Samuel 10:25). But Samuel himself carried on a spoken ministry and left no written collection of prophecies.

1000 to 922 B.C.: The beginning of the monarchy. Only at this stage, centuries after the exodus, did the process of committing oral traditions to writing get seriously underway. The royal court of David and Solomon, and the temple that Solomon built, provided educated men with the time and resources for this work. What some scholars call the "primary history"—the great national history of Israel running from Genesis through 2 Kings—began to take shape as men transposed oral traditions into texts. Even so, the written output in this period may have been meager. In any case, the writing and rewriting, adding and subtracting, editing and rearranging was to continue for centuries.

While many authors and editors worked on the narrative and legal material that evolved into the Pentateuch, these first five books became associated with Moses, who had played the central role in leading the people from Egypt and mediating God's covenant to them in the desert. Thus the Pentateuch came to be called "the Books of Moses." In time these first five books were thought to have flowed from his pen.

Priests and people had been singing prayers at regional sanctuaries and in the Jerusalem temple. Now some leaders, probably at the temple, began to gather these prayer songs, or "psalms," and write them down. The psalm collection became associated with David, who probably gave an initial impetus to the project. Exactly how the book of Psalms (the "Psalter") developed is a matter of much debate. But it certainly grew over centuries. The collection had not yet reached final form in Jesus' day, a millennium later (first-century scrolls found near the Dead Sea show that the exact number and order of the psalms was still not yet quite settled in the first century).

Also during this period, learned people in Jerusalem began to collect wise sayings. Over a long period, this collection evolved into the book of Proverbs. The collection came to be associated with an early patron, Solomon—as did some later "wisdom" books (Ecclesiastes, Wisdom).

922 to 721 B.C.: From the dividing of the kingdom to the fall of the northern kingdom. Drawing on oral traditions, religious leaders in the northern kingdom, Israel (and perhaps also in the southern kingdom, Judah), wrote portions of the book now called Deuteronomy (chapters 5–11, 28). These writings, which took shape more than three centuries after Moses' death, contain instructions that Moses laid out on behalf of God for his people.

At the same time, new oral material from prophets such as Amos, Hosea, and Micah was entering the communal tradition. Their disciples remembered and preserved their words in writing, but the continuing emphasis on the spoken word is seen in the primarily oral nature of their public ministries. The notable prophets Elijah and Elisha did not leave behind any written works of their own, but their dramatic acts were remembered. (see 1 Kings 17–19, 21; 2 Kings 1–8, 13).

721 to 587 B.C.: From the fall of the northern kingdom to the fall of the southern kingdom. The portion of Deuteronomy which had so far been written now came to public attention in the southern kingdom, where it caused a great deal of soul-searching (see 2 Kings 22:3-20). This may have been the first time that God's word in written form played a decisive role in Israelite history.

The draft of Deuteronomy confronted Israel with a stark choice of obedience or disobedience to God, leading to either blessing or destruction. Influenced by this outlook, the authors at work on the "primary history" of Israel highlighted Israel's experience of this dynamic of faithfulness-and-blessing or unfaithfulness-and-destruction. Because of this influence, modern scholars call the books from Joshua to 2 Kings the "deuteronomist" history.

Despite this compositional activity, the spoken word continued to be the preeminent vehicle of God's communication with his people. In oral proclamation prophets brought God's word to bear on the declining fortunes of the southern kingdom, although their prophecies were soon written down (Isaiah of Jerusalem [Isaiah 1–39]; the prophet Jeremiah).

587 to 539 B.C.: Exile in Babylon. This period of suffering bore fruit in a profound revitalization of God's people. Prophecies delivered by Ezekiel and by an anonymous prophet or prophets whose words were collected with those of Isaiah (see Isaiah 40–55) spurred repentance and renewal among the exiles.

Authors and editors working during the exile brought the Pentateuch close to completion—more than seven centuries after the events. At this stage, scholars think, the editors added the creation and primeval stories at the beginning of Genesis (see Genesis 1–11), drawn in part from older Mesopotamian literature. They fashioned the patriarchal narratives (see Genesis 12–50) to give the exiles the hope that God's promises of land and blessing to their ancestors would yet be fulfilled in their own lives. They revised the laws of the Pentateuch to make a workable constitution for their renewed community, if and when they were allowed to return to their homeland. With a chastened view of Israel's failure to heed God's word, editors completed the historical books from Joshua to 2 Kings, bringing out the lessons to be learned from the moral and spiritual failures which had led to Israel's destruction.

539 to 333 B.C.: Reestablishment in the land of Israel under Persian rule. Through prophets such as Haggai and Malachi, the spoken word continued to be a vital means of divine guidance for God's people (now called Jews) who returned from Babylon. A prophet or prophets whose names are unknown spoke words of encouragement that were preserved as the last part of Isaiah (see Isaiah 56–66). Thus the book of Isaiah contains an entire tradition, spanning some two hundred years, from the mid-eighth to the mid-sixth centuries.

Leaders of the returning exiles composed accounts of their own time (the books of Ezra and Nehemiah). The same circle of religious leaders also produced a revised history of the pre-exilic period (1 and 2 Chronicles), bringing out lessons that steered the renewed community toward trust in God and a life centered on worship in the temple.

333 to 100 B.C.: Greek-speaking emperors, Jewish revolt and autonomy. Two authors produced works that probed life's unpredictability and inequalities (Ecclesiastes, Job). These authors used traditional material—proverbs and wise sayings—to produce critiques of traditional views. As pagan Greek culture spread throughout the Near East, other authors drew from wisdom traditions to reassure their readers that the

God of Israel and his law are the sources of a truly successful life (Wisdom, Sirach). Using background and characters from oral traditions, other authors wrote stories that gave beleaguered Jews courage and hope and provided examples for living (Esther, Judith, Tobit).

When Greek-speaking emperors in Syria began to persecute the Jews, devout persons elaborated on oral legends about a wise man named Daniel and supplemented the accounts with prophetic visions, producing a book to strengthen the Jews' faithfulness to God (Daniel). The persecution and the successful Jewish revolt against it were recorded in two somewhat parallel accounts (1 and 2 Maccabees).

5 B.C. to A.D. 30: Life, death, and resurrection of Jesus of Nazareth. It is a fact of immense significance that Jesus, the central actor in the entire sweep of biblical events, did not write anything. He communicated his message entirely through actions and spoken words. Jesus drew around himself men and women to observe his preaching and healings, his manner of life, his death and resurrection. He left the writing to them.

A.D. 30 to 66 : From Jesus' departure until the death of the apostles Peter and Paul. After Jesus' departure, his followers focused not on writing down their recollections of him but on making him known through preaching and personal contact. Thus all the reports of Jesus' life and message passed through a short but crucial period of oral tradition. During this period, which lasted for some three or four decades, the apostles constantly shaped their reminiscences of Jesus to serve the purpose of helping men and women believe in him and follow him.

At the same time, it may well be that some Christians began to put some of Jesus' words and deeds into writing as early as the first decade after his departure. It seems that a written collection of his sayings developed, although it probably lacked an extended narrative framework. Many scholars refer to this no longer extant document as "Q"—for the German word Quelle, meaning "source." A few scholars think there was an Aramaic draft of some material later enlarged into Matthew's Gospel.

Meanwhile Paul and other early leaders wrote letters to communities and individuals. Often these writers made explicit references to the preaching and pastoral instruction that had already become traditional in the early Church (see 1 Corinthians 2:1-5; Galatians 1:6-9; 2:1-2; 1 Thessalonians 1:4-5; Titus 1:9). They incorporated material from the Christian communities' oral traditions: hymns (see Philippians 2:6-11), confessions of faith (see 1 Corinthians 12:3), baptismal sermons (see 1 Peter 1), and moral teaching (see 1 Thessalonians 4:1-8).

A.D. 66 to the end of the first century. Now the apostolic traditions about Jesus were put into definitive written form. On the basis of recollections of Jesus that had been focused by decades of preaching and enriched by reflection, and with the help of some written sources, several authors composed narratives covering Jesus' public activity, death, and resurrection. These are the written Gospels—the preaching of Jesus and the early Church in written form.

On the basis of their acquaintance with the apostles Peter and Paul, associates applied the apostles' teaching to circumstances a generation or so after their deaths (2 Peter, 1 and 2 Timothy, Titus). These letters were further crystallizations of apostolic traditions.

Close to the end of the century, a visionary named John wrote a vivid and mysterious portrayal of the conflict between the kingdom of God and the forces of evil from Jesus' resurrection until his return (Revelation). The book draws together countless strands of historical and prophetic traditions from the entire biblical period to show that God will ultimately fulfill his purposes for the human race through Jesus Christ.

Spoken Words

One feature that stands forth prominently from this brief survey is the large part played by the spoken word. In many cases, the word of God was spoken long before it was written. Narratives, teachings, laws, prayers, poems, proverbs, prophecies—a great deal originated in oral form. In the Old Testament period, even as parts of the oral tradition were being set in writing (the histories), new sources of oral tradition constantly arose (the prophets). After the Old Testament books were written, a

---

What Languages Was the Bible Written In?

The Old Testament was originally composed in Hebrew with a few exceptions: (1) Tobit, part of Ezra, and part of Daniel were written in Aramaic. (2) Judith, 2 Maccabees, Wisdom, part of Daniel, and portions of Esther were written in Greek. Written in Hebrew or Aramaic but preserved today only in Greek: 1 Maccabees and Baruch and portions of Tobit and Sirach. The New Testament was written entirely in Greek.

new wave of oral material arose—the apostolic preaching about Jesus, along with early Christian hymns, creeds, and instruction.

The Bible's origins in spoken words does not mean that the biblical narratives are historically unreliable. Ancient cultures placed a high value on the spoken word. Traditions were carefully guarded. Memory was tenacious. It was possible for accounts to be passed on intact over long periods of time. But the oral nature of the biblical traditions gives them a particular character. Unlike written material, oral reports are constantly shaped in the telling for each particular audience. Selecting, emphasizing, simplifying, rearranging, dramatizing, explaining—each time a speaker presents his or her material, he or she tries to make it relevant to the listeners. The speaker's goal is always to say something that is of immediate importance; anything outside that focus tends to drop away. In my family's oral tradition there is a recollection of why my grandfather came to the United States from Italy. The family story does not include general information about the social and political situation in Italy or America at the time.

Oral traditions change. Different versions develop. Consequently the biblical authors who put oral traditions into written form often had available more than one rendition of a particular incident, prayer, proverb, or other material. In some cases, the authors wove more than one strand of oral material into their finished product. For example, the authors of Genesis incorporated various traditions of God's promises to Abraham and Sarah into the book of Genesis (see Genesis 12, 15, 17, 18). They used these variant oral traditions to create a larger story about how God called the couple to believe his promises even though the fulfillment seemed unlikely. Despite the authors' masterful work, the finished product contains repetitions and inconsistencies—the marks of its complicated history. The reader who is puzzled by these features will find it useful to know that they probably stem from varying oral traditions.

Authors Unknown

Secondly, our rapid survey of the Bible's development highlights the fact that when we open the Bible we must leave behind our modern concept of authorship. We do not know who most of the biblical authors were. The names of Moses, David, Solomon, and Isaiah all became associated with collections of material that continued to grow long after their deaths. In the New Testament, Matthew's association with the first Gospel, Paul's with the "pastoral epistles" (1 and 2 Timothy and Titus), and Peter's with 2 Peter may be similar ways in which later material was connected with earlier authoritative figures.

Ancient conventions of authorship were simply different from ours. In ancient times it was acceptable to place new writing under the name of a person of the past. The fact that we do not follow such a convention today does not diminish the inspiration and authority of the biblical writings. Thus the Catholic Church leaves scholars free to investigate the identity of the actual authors of the biblical books. Scholarly speculation about authorship does not jeopardize the value of the biblical writings, for regardless of authorship, they authentically convey the traditions of Israel and the early Church. It was precisely to affirm this authenticity that the ancient editors masked the identity of the authors and placed their works under the names of great figures of the tradition such as Moses and Solomon.

Rewriting and Editing

Thirdly, from our survey we can see that the Bible fixes in writing the traditions of Israel and the Church at many stages of tradition. Writing gives oral traditions a fixed form. Yet even after being written down, the biblical writings continued to be part of a living tradition. They belonged not to a museum but to a community that enjoyed an ongoing relationship with God, who was unfolding further stages of his plan. In the Old Testament period God led the people of Israel to a deeper and deeper understanding of himself. As they experienced God's saving help and faithfulness, his correction and discipline, they grew in awe, love, and devotion. Vatican Council II called the process "the divine pedagogy"—God's course of instruction for his people (*Dogmatic Constitution on Divine Revelation*, section 14).

Signs of the ongoing development of traditions are especially apparent in the Old Testament. Even as the books began to take shape, the people of Israel saw new depths of meaning in past events. Earlier ideas were clarified and enlarged. Old instructions were applied to new situations.

Because those who handed on the traditions venerated what they received, they often kept what they had received even while modifying it. There was an interplay between careful preservation on the one hand and new interpretation on the other. A view expressed in absolute terms in one place might be qualified by placing a differing view in another place—or even right alongside it. As a result, the library of the Old Testament contains both older and newer views of events and different perspectives on various issues.

A major example is the teaching about divine reward and retribution. The view of God's judgment emphasized in the books stretching from Deuteronomy to 2 Kings is subjected to a severe critique in Job and Ecclesiastes. Bound together in the Bible, the different perspectives modify each other. The assertion stands that God does make his judgments felt in this world (the view of the books from Deuteronomy to Kings), but this assertion is qualified by the rejoinder that he does not always or necessarily execute judgment in this world (the contention of Job and Ecclesiastes). Thus the meanings of various authors are not canceled out but are balanced out, revealing truths that are complex, even paradoxical.

The process of reinterpretation and reapplication can be seen in every type of writing in the Bible. Here are a few more examples.

The patriarchal stories (Genesis 12–50), which were the stories of God's promises to Abraham, Isaac, and Jacob were reshaped so that they might speak the word of God to later generations living in different circumstances. Thus:

- Before they went into Egypt, the descendants of the patriarchs were semi-nomads living in small, family groups. The stories of God's dealing with their ancestors assured these defenseless people that God had called them, had placed them under his protection, had put his blessing on them.
- During the tribal period in Canaan, these stories functioned as reminders that all the tribes who regarded the patriarchs as common ancestors shared a common call from God—and thus a commitment to defend each other.
- For the Israelites who were deported to Babylon, God's promises of the land of Canaan to Abraham, Isaac, and Jacob nourished their hope that, even though they had failed to keep the terms of the covenant with God, God, out of his

unconditional love and faithfulness, would care for them and restore them to their land.

Legal material in the Pentateuch was adapted to changing circumstances and deepening understanding. Rules about animal sacrifice and appropriate places of worship developed over time. In many cases, changes were incorporated into the legal material associated with Moses. It was as if the American people modified the Constitution not by adding amendments but by subtly rewriting the body of the Constitution, so that later alterations looked as though they had been written by James Madison and Alexander Hamilton.

The books of prayer and reflection were expanded. By adding new introductions, later contributors sometimes added new levels of meaning. For example:

- Many psalms began as songs to be prayed publicly in the temple. As they were gathered into the book of Psalms, they came to have a second use as prayers for individual meditation to accompany the study of the Torah. Psalm 1 was placed at the beginning of the collection to highlight this purpose.
- Proverbs arose in everyday life as people distilled their experience of the world into pithy sayings. Editors combined these folk sayings (see Proverbs 10–24) with reflections on God as the ultimate source of wisdom and on his law as the great channel of wisdom for human beings (see Proverbs 1–9). Thus the book of Proverbs now has a complex message: wisdom is to be sought from both judicious observation of life (the source of proverbs) and from God, especially through studying his law. We grow wise both by exercising common sense and by listening to God's word.

The prophets sometimes expressed views that were in tension with the tradition. For example, compare Exodus 34:6-7 with Ezekiel 18. Israelite anticipations that God would execute justice in the world by bringing judgment on pagan nations (see Zechariah 14:12-15) were juxtaposed with prophecies that God would call the pagan nations to himself in a new covenant (see Isaiah 19:19-25).

Implications

The Bible's long, complex process of development—from oral traditions, through writing, rewriting, and editing—has implications that we will explore in the following chapters.

- While the historical books of the Bible recount actual events, they are not history in the modern sense (chapter four).
- The source of unity in the biblical books, produced by so many hands over so many centuries, lies in the one God who was interacting all through this time with Israel and the Church (chapter five).
- As a crystallization of the traditions of a community, the Bible belongs to the community within which it developed. It can be understood only from within that community (chapter six).
- To be understood properly, the Bible needs to be read both with an awareness of its history and with a grasp of its central focus, Jesus Christ (chapter seven).

Chapter Four

Did It Really Happen?
The Historical Reliability of the Bible

The Bible is historical. It is concerned with what God has done in history and it communicates a great deal of historical information. But at no point is it quite like modern historical writing, and at some points it is quite different. The biblical writers belonged to cultures that wrote about the past differently from historians today. The historical material in the Bible bears all the marks of the cultures in which it was written.

Ancient historians were different from modern ones in regard to their *approach* and in regard to their *resources*.

- *Approach.* Modern historians try to present the context of events. They examine political, economic, military, and social factors. They trace the development of individuals, institutions, and ideas. They try to view conflicts from the perspectives of both sides. Ancient historians, by contrast, were less concerned with the background and context of events or with the development of personalities and groups or with exploring competing points of view. Their chief concern was to narrate events in ways that exhibited their meaning for their readers. To accomplish this, they felt freer than modern writers to shape, omit, combine, and supply details. For example, they considered it acceptable to supplement a person's speech with words of their own in order to express the speaker's views more fully. From a modern point of view, ancient historians' approach may seem like an inferior way to write history. We would like something more fully and purely factual. From the ancient point of view, however, a neutral narrative would be a worthless exercise. The ancient historian would ask, "If we remember events because they continue to have meaning for us, why should we refrain from recounting them in ways that highlight their meaning?"

- *Resources.* While ancient historians could draw on historical sources that have since disappeared, they did not have access to the accumulations of literary and archeological data, the museums of artifacts, the vast numbers of books, journals, tapes, and videos that modern historians can draw on. Typically, their sources consisted of oral traditions and a few documents. Thus, in many cases ancient writers could not discover details of time and place and quantity or the precise words that had been spoken. Often they were not able to quote verbatim, cite exact figures, or report exactly when and in what sequence events occurred.

As a result, the biblical histories leave questions unanswered. When was Joseph taken into slavery in Egypt? What was the name of the Pharaoh who oppressed the Hebrews? Did Moses' views of God change over the years? What was the cultural, linguistic, and political background of the peoples that the Israelites confronted in Palestine? How long did Jesus' public life last? Did *his* thinking change over time? Did he attack the merchants in the Jerusalem temple at the beginning or the end of his ministry? What were his precise words of blessing over the bread and wine on the night before his death? The biblical authors do not give us answers or give us different answers, because these matters did not seem important to them or because they had no way of knowing or because their sources gave *them* different answers.

The biblical authors were people of their time and place. They worked within the limitations of their culture. Yet they were honest writers who strove to communicate the truth. Their narratives do not contain lies or deceptions. The historical writing in the Bible compares very well with other history-writing of the period. Whatever the difficulties and shortcomings of the human authors, God was able to work through them to establish a reliable testimony to his deeds and to communicate his message.

There is no single answer to the question, "How historically reliable is the Bible?" for the biblical narratives are of different types. Here are a few remarks about their historical value.

Genesis 1–11. The stories in the early chapters of Genesis are not historical accounts. These stories combine mythical, legendary, and historical elements in forms familiar to people in the ancient Near East but corresponding to little in our modern Western culture. Perhaps the closest parallel in our experience is the parable. The parable is an imaginary story that communicates a truth and spurs us to think. The similarity between Genesis and parables is only partial, however, since parables are fictional, while some actual events do lie behind the Genesis accounts, even though they are not conveyed in straightforward historical or scientific language.

The Catholic Church makes no claim that the early chapters of Genesis are historical or scientific in the modern sense of the word. As the Pontifical Biblical Commission wrote in 1948, these narratives "relate in simple and figurative language, adapted to the understanding of mankind at a lower stage of development, the fundamental truths presupposed by the economy of salvation, as well as the popular description of the beginnings of the human race" (quoted by George T. Montague, *Understanding the Bible*, page 102).

Confusing Genesis 1–11 with history has had unhappy consequences. Thinking they are defending the Bible against theories that contradict it, many Christians have resisted evolutionary explanations of the development of species, especially *Homo sapiens*. But the Genesis stories are not concerned with biological processes. This is apparent, for example, when the narrator of Genesis offers two different descriptions of the process by which God brought humans into existence. Chapter one states that God "created" us by a simple command (1:27), using a Hebrew word that never refers to making one thing from another. Yet chapter two says that God "formed" a man from dust and "made" a woman from the man's rib, using words elsewhere applied to making clay pots and houses (2:7, 22). Evidently the narrator was intent on communicating *that* God created humans; *how* God did it was not part of his message. Since the Genesis accounts do not intend to convey scientific or historical information in the modern sense, they are in no danger of being contradicted by scientific or historical findings. No biological discovery can ever disprove the Genesis message that God created the human race, since in creating us God could have chosen any process that biologists might ever discover.

Recognizing the parable-like quality of the Genesis accounts keeps us from getting hung up in futile controversies. This frees us to focus on the meaning of the accounts: God created;

humans turned away from God; God brings judgment on sin, but remains kindly disposed toward humankind.

Genesis 12–50. Portions of the accounts of Abraham and Sarah and the other ancestors of Israel are very ancient. A sign of the stories' early origin is their portrayal of the patriarchs as following a semi-nomadic lifestyle: the patriarchs live in tents, travel in small family groups, get into disagreements over wells and pasturage. This lifestyle had been left behind by the later generations that wrote the accounts. Archaeologists have brought to light evidence of the patriarchs' way of life; for example, they have confirmed that at one period in Mesopotamia (modern Iraq) it was the practice for a childless wife to give her female servant to her husband as a concubine to produce offspring in her name (Genesis 16:1-4).

But as we saw in chapter three, later generations seem to have heavily reworked the patriarchal accounts in order to show their relevance for their own times. Much of the patriarchal narratives may not have been written down until the end of the southern monarchy and the exile in Babylon, more than seven centuries after the fact. It is doubtful that the stories passed through such a long period of oral retelling without significant changes. Some of the patriarchal material may be regarded as legendary.

These stories should be read for their meaning, regardless of questions about their historicity. We know that God made promises to the ancestors of Israel, and the stories of his interactions with them are rich with significance for us today.

Exodus, Leviticus, Numbers, Deuteronomy, Joshua, Judges. Here too the accounts went through a considerable period of oral transmission before reaching papyrus. Scholars raise many questions. Did *all* the descendants of Abraham, Isaac, and Jacob immigrate to Egypt and later experience the exodus, as described in Exodus—or did those who came out of Egypt join up with others who had not gone into Egypt and bring them into the covenant that God had made with them at Sinai? Was there really an Israelite conquest of Canaan—or did semi-nomadic Israelites gradually settle down and take up farming, perhaps bringing into their tribal association peasants who were already in the land? Questions such as these arise not only from an examination of archaeological evidence, which does not always confirm the biblical accounts, but also from a careful reading of the various strands of material preserved in the Bible. The book of Joshua portrays an Israelite conquest of Canaan, but the book of Judges shows the Canaanites still in control of the cities.

Whatever the answers to these sorts of questions, the basic facts are secure. God led some enslaved people out of Egypt, revealed himself to them, made a covenant with them, protected—and corrected—them in the desert, and brought about their settlement in Canaan. We may let the historians argue over the details, while we explore the meaning of these events for us.

1 and 2 Samuel. These biblical narratives are grounded on more recent recollections and on written sources. The accounts of Samuel and Saul may have been put in writing within a generation of the events. The wealth of detail about David far exceeds that concerning any later king in Israel. The narrative of the succession to David's throne (see 2 Samuel 11–20; 1 Kings 1–2) is a masterpiece of historical writing. Yet materials from varied oral sources have been combined in the books of Samuel, as can be seen from the multiple accounts of how David became king (see 1 Samuel 16:1-13; 16:14-23; 17; 1 Samuel 18:1–2 Samuel 2:5).

1 and 2 Kings. The authors of Kings worked with written sources such as palace archives. Beginning with Kings, details in the biblical narratives can be checked against sources outside the Bible (before this period Israel is very rarely mentioned in the records of other nations). For example, some accounts in Kings can be correlated with records from ancient Assyria, an empire that played a large and destructive role in the history of Israel. The Assyrian accounts support the historical nature of Kings, although they do not always line up perfectly. Clearly the biblical authors were telling the story from their own point of view (as were the Assyrian scribes!).

1 and 2 Chronicles. The books of Chronicles cover much the same ground as 2 Samuel and 1 and 2 Kings. In fact, the authors of Chronicles used Samuel and Kings as their main sources of information. If you set the accounts side by side, you will see how the authors of Chronicles reworked material in Samuel and Kings. The authors of Chronicles respected their sources but felt free to add and subtract in order to help readers of their own day see what the historical events meant for them.

Ezra, Nehemiah, Maccabees. These histories were written on the basis of recent recollections and numerous documents. Still, they are not modern histories, and scholars find much to puzzle over; for example, the chronologies of events. The author of 2 Maccabees gave his own account of the period recorded in 1 Maccabees 1–7. Again, setting the two accounts side by side, you can see how each writer shaped his narrative to emphasize certain points—sometimes different ones (the author of 2 Maccabees is not so admiring of the Maccabee family as is the author of 1 Maccabees).

Ruth, Tobit, Judith, and Esther. These books reflect historical situations to varying degrees, and perhaps even some actual events, especially Ruth. But they are largely imaginative works written to provide models of behavior and encouragement.

The Gospels. In order to understand the historical nature of the Gospels, it is useful to distinguish three phases:

1. **Jesus with his disciples.** The disciples observed and listened to their master and remembered what he said and did, but they did not write anything.
2. **Oral tradition.** After Jesus' departure, guided by the Holy Spirit, the disciples pondered his life and death in light of his resurrection and spoke about him to others.
3. **The writing of the Gospels.** Several writers composed the Gospels from the oral traditions about Jesus and some written sources (no longer extant). Scholars disagree about the extent to which any of Jesus' original disciples contributed to the writing.

Since at least some of the Gospel writers (sometimes called "evangelists") were not eyewitnesses of Jesus' ministry, we may ask what sources they drew on. Scholars find it reasonable to suppose that:

• The Gospel writers inherited oral accounts of Jesus that had been shaped by years of preaching and pastoral care. As the incidents of Jesus' life and the traditions of his teaching were handed on, there would have been a tendency for details that did not serve these purposes to drop out. Much of the material may have come to the evangelists shorn of names, places, dates, secondary dialogue, or information about the occasions.

- The accounts may have reached the evangelists in the form of single incidents or short groups of incidents and small units of teaching. The original chronology of Jesus' ministry may no longer have been remembered, although the oral traditions do seem to have passed on a connected narrative of Jesus' last days and hours.

- Handed on by different groups in different places, the traditions had become somewhat varied. Particular incidents in Jesus' life and elements of his teaching were remembered in somewhat different forms (compare the miracle of loaves and fish in Luke 9:10-17 and John 6:1-14).

- The evangelists probably had access to some written collections of Jesus' words and actions.

From Oral Traditions to Written Gospels

"After the Ascension of the Lord the Apostles handed on to their hearers what He had said and done. This they did with that clearer understanding which they enjoyed after they had been instructed by the glorious events of Christ's risen life and taught by the light of the Spirit of truth. The sacred authors wrote the four Gospels, selecting some things from the many which had been handed on by word of mouth or in writing, reducing some of them to a synthesis, explaining some things in view of the situation of their churches, and preserving the form of proclamation but always in such fashion that they told us the honest truth about Jesus." *Dogmatic Constitution on Divine Revelation*, section 19.

Like those who handed on the traditions about Jesus by word of mouth, the Gospel writers wished to help people believe in Jesus and follow him faithfully. They were not university professors writing academic histories but men with evangelistic and pastoral purposes. Through the particular traditions they had access to and the particular inspirations they received, the Gospel writers developed different visions of Jesus. In writing, they were also responding to different pastoral needs.

The result was four distinct portraits of Jesus. The sequence of events is somewhat different in each, probably because each evangelist created a chronological framework for the smaller units of material that had come to him in the tradition. Thus the chronologies of the Gospels, with the exception of the accounts of Jesus' last supper, suffering, and death, may not represent the order in which the events actually occurred. Rather the chronologies serve to structure the evangelists' portraits of Jesus.

There are similarities between the Gospels but also differences. Some of the similarities are due to parallels in the traditions upon which the writers drew. Some similarities are due to the fact that a couple of the Gospel writers used the work of another writer. Who used whom is a matter of disagreement. Most scholars think that Matthew and Luke both used Mark, that they also had another written source in common ("Q"—see page 37), and that each had an additional source of information. A few scholars, however, maintain that Luke used Matthew and Mark used Luke. Differences may be due to divergences in the oral traditions and to the evangelists' unique treatments of the traditions.

How historically reliable was the outcome? Obviously, like

the rest of biblical history, the Gospels are not written as modern history. But there is every reason to think that those who handed on the oral traditions and those who committed them to writing communicated a genuine picture of Jesus. I can only mention a few pieces of evidence here.

First, the evangelists did not manufacture material to deal with the greatest pastoral and theological crisis that the Church faced after Jesus' departure. Should gentiles be admitted directly into the Christian community or did they have to become Jews first, undertaking to follow the Mosaic law? This question touched on the Church's basic understanding of Jesus and its own identity. Since the issue did not arise during Jesus' lifetime, there was nothing in the traditions about him that directly answered it. It would have been tempting for those who preached or wrote down the traditions about Jesus to make up some statements by him that would resolve the controversy. But they did not—although the Gospel writers did highlight incidents in which Jesus had dealings with non-Jews.

Faithful Portraits of Jesus

"Holy Mother Church has firmly and with absolute constancy held, and continues to hold, that the four Gospels ...whose historical character the Church unhesitatingly asserts, faithfully hand on what Jesus Christ, while living among men, really did and taught for their eternal salvation." *Dogmatic Constitution on Divine Revelation*, section 19.

Second, the evangelists retained material that had lost its original relevance. During his ministry, Jesus frequently confronted questions about how to keep the Sabbath. By the time the evangelists wrote, this was no longer a burning issue for most Christians, who were not Jews. Nevertheless, the Church continued to pass on many accounts of Jesus' controversies with fellow Jews about Sabbath observance, and the evangelists incorporated them in the Gospels.

Third, they reported incidents that put Jesus' closest followers in an unfavorable light, such as Peter's denial of Jesus (see John 18:15-18, 25-27). Since those close followers went on to become the leaders of the early Church, there would have been a strong motivation for erasing the many accounts of their incomprehension, resistance, lack of faith, and infidelity to Jesus. But the Gospels have not been so "cleansed."

Thus while the evangelists, like the preachers of the gospel before them, reshaped the traditions about Jesus to serve people in their own day, they were honest men who did not falsify the traditions they had received. Guided by the Spirit, the evangelists produced accounts of Jesus that faithfully brought out his meaning for later Christians.

Given the way the material about Jesus was handed on by word of mouth, the Gospels do not necessarily give us Jesus' precise words. But they give us Jesus' words as they were recalled and repeated in the preaching of the early Church, by those who had known him and were inspired by the Spirit. The Gospel reports thus bring us close to Jesus' words and deeds— as close, say, as the Corinthians were able to get, who listened to Paul's preaching about Jesus in the year A.D. 51.

Since the differences between the Gospels are rooted in different oral traditions, it is not possible to produce a neat synthesis of them, although countless people have made the attempt over the centuries. But the differences between the Gospels need not make us feel that they are unhistorical. The fourfold Gospel tradition creates a three-dimensional picture of Jesus; it allows us to see Jesus from different angles. Although the differences between the Gospels might have suggested historical unreliability, the Church has regarded the fourfold Gospel as a treasure rather than an embarrassment. In the face of an attempt in the second century by a Syrian Christian named Tatian to synthesize the four Gospels into a single narrative, the Church insisted on preserving the distinct written versions of the apostolic preaching about Jesus.

Acts of the Apostles. Archaeologists have found much to confirm the historical nature of Luke's history of the early Church. The titles of government officials, the position of political boundaries, local customs—Luke gets the details right. Careful investigation of the text suggests that Luke had various sources to draw on, and that he dealt carefully with them. Yet, like the authors of the Old Testament histories, he told of events as an ancient, not a modern, historian. Studies of ancient biography and history writing show that Luke followed the conventions of the time—and that his account stands up well by comparison with other works of his time.

Chapter Five

Whose Words Are These?

The Bible's Divine and Human Dimensions

God acted in the lives of the people of Israel. He acted above all through Jesus of Nazareth. He continued to act in the early Church. At every step, God was revealing himself. In his self-revelation, deeds and words worked in tandem.

Through his involvement in people's lives, God demonstrated his compassion and power, graciousness and justice, faithfulness and generosity. But the events through which God worked could effectively reveal him only if accompanied by words of explanation. Otherwise no one would have perceived the meaning of his actions. The sight of some slaves crossing marshy ground on their way into the Sinai desert or of a man hanging on a cross—what did these events mean? Without interpretation, no observer could have known that God was rescuing slaves in order to make a covenant with them or that he was receiving his Son's offering of himself as an atonement for the world's sins. God's words were needed to explain his deeds.

Conversely, God confirmed his words by his deeds. The return of Jewish exiles from Babylon and their rebuilding of the Jerusalem temple (see Ezra 1–6) fulfilled God's promise that he would bring them home and restore them (see Jeremiah 30). The healings that the Spirit accomplished through the apostles demonstrated the reliability of their preaching about Jesus (see Acts 3–4).

From events-with-interpretation and words-confirmed, the Bible came into being. The historical books began to form around events in which God's hand was glimpsed. The prophetic books preserved the messages of men who presented God's view of his people's condition and alerted them to what he was going to do about it. As we have seen, the deeds and the words were remembered, handed on orally, put into writing, rewritten, and edited. The Bible is the sedimentation of this process, laid down over many centuries. It bears witness to God's self-revelation in word and deed.

The purpose of God's self-revelation was to bring people into relationship with himself. Naturally, the writings that arose through his interaction with his people have the same purpose. The Bible so well reflects the process of God's revealing himself and acting among people that it continues to be the instrument of his self-revealing and acting. Through the Bible, God continues to draw us to himself.

Before my wife and I got married, I used to write her letters. She lived just on the other side of town, but that seemed a long way off. So I wrote her all sorts of notes, poems, lists, and ponderings about my life, what I thought of her, what I hoped for. Somewhere in a closet she has them stashed away in a box. To her, they have some meaning. I doubt that they would be of much interest to anyone else. The letters have little intrinsic value. They were not written to supply material for anyone composing an anthology of literature or a social history of twentieth-century America. Basically, they are love letters.

Basically, that is what the Bible is, too. The Bible is God's means of communication with human beings. In the Bible, God has shown us the kind of person he is and what he is about in the world so that we may live in a relationship with him. The purpose of the Bible is not that we should simply have a lot of information concerning what God has said and done, but that, through this information, we would know his love for us. God gives us the book in order to give us himself.

Thus the Bible achieves its purpose only in the context of a love relationship between God and us. Historians can troll in the biblical books for information about ancient Near Eastern events; linguists can sift it for specimens of ancient languages. These uses are fine, as far as they go. But to treat the Bible only as a source of historical or linguistic information, or merely as an anthology of notable literature or even a compendium of religious wisdom, misses the point. In the Bible, God wishes to meet us and speak to us.

Truths Revealed

By his interventions in history and his words of explanation, God has made clear and accessible some truths that we could have discovered by natural means. God had already revealed himself by creating. Without special revelation, we could reason from effect to cause—from the existence, order, and beauty of the universe to the activity of One who is powerful and wise (see Romans 1:19-20). From an examination of ourselves we could reach a conclusion about the goodness of God, since conscience, the moral compass in us, is evidence of a just creator.

But this kind of reasoning is difficult, and most of us are not inclined to think long and hard about such matters. Moreover, we are easily confused by the cacophony of voices in the world around us, promoting divergent views ("nothing certain can be known about God," "there is no God," "there are many gods"). Our inclination to evil distorts our reasoning. So it is helpful that God has made apparent to us through revelation even those basic truths about himself that we might grasp the basis of what he has already shown through creation.

Through his plan of salvation, however, God has revealed more to us than we could have known by our reasoning. He has shown us that we are designed for relationship with him (part of the meaning of being created in his image—Genesis 1:26). He has revealed that his saving plan centers on the incarnation, death, and resurrection of his Son (a "mystery," or secret now unveiled by God—Ephesians 1:9). Without his telling us, we could not have known that God has destined us, body and soul, for unending life with himself. Nor could we have known him to be one God who is yet Father, Son, and Holy Spirit.

Inspiration

Who but God is able to identify God's activities in the midst of human affairs? Who but God is able to know God's evaluation of human beings and their circumstances? Who but God is able to predict the course of action that God is going to take? Who but God is able to reveal the overarching plan that God is pursuing through human history? Obviously, no one but God!

Thus if the Bible does all these things, it must in some sense be *God's* word. That, of course, is just what the Church claims the Bible to be. But, then, the *human* authors of Scripture have written *God's* words. How is that possible? The Christian answer is that God guided the authors and editors of the biblical books—he "inspired" them. As they thought, wrote, and edited, God communicated himself and his plans to their minds and hearts.

"Holy Mother Church ... accepts as sacred and canonical the books of the Old and the New Testaments, whole and entire, with all their parts, on the ground that, written under the inspiration of the Holy Spirit ...they have God as their author." *Dogmatic Constitution on Divine Revelation*, section 11.

Inspiration involved a mysterious cooperation between God and human beings. God guided the perceiving and thinking, the speaking and writing and editing, of these members of Israel and the early Church so that their words would convey the message that he wished to convey.

How the infinite God interacted with his finite creatures to accomplish this is beyond our understanding. Somehow God uttered his words in the depths of the authors and editors—at the level of mind and heart where humans hunger for God. God guided them by revealing himself to them. By his Spirit, he directed them not by merely putting thoughts in their heads but by communicating his life, his truth to them.

"We would be misled if revelation were taken to mean primarily certain facts or truths about God and religion. Revelation is primarily God's personal communication of himself to his children. You might know everything about God, but not know God; you would not have received his revelation. God's plan is part of revelation, but it is the second part. The first part is God himself." Jerome Kodell, OSB, *The Catholic Bible Study Handbook*, page 5.

The reception of inspiration does not seem to have required any particular mental or emotional condition on the part of the human participants. Certainly the authors and editors of the biblical books were not of any one personality type. Their works display a variety of temperaments and moods—and also a variety of abilities. Among the biblical authors are theological geniuses, master storytellers, and world-class historians; but there are also some merely so-so poets, some writers of labored prose, and an editor who acknowledged his own limitations (see 2 Maccabees 15:38). God inspired them all.

Inspiration was not divine dictation. The human authors were fully authors. The thoroughly human quality of their writing is apparent in every line they produced, no matter how sublime or profound. Their works were fully their own. Yet, at the same time, their works were fully inspired by God. The result is the words of God in the words of human beings.

The mystery of inspiration is all the more profound for being non-miraculous, in the sense that it did not involve God's overriding human functioning. God did not suspend the human participants' human nature in order to speak through them. As Dom Celestin Charlier has written, "Biblical writers wrote as other men do, and left the imprint of their personality on their work. For the most part they were not even conscious that they were inspired. Inspiration must not therefore be thought of as a *substitution* of God's action for the normal activity of the writer" (*The Christian Approach to the Bible*, page 210).

In whatever way it operated, God's inspiration of the human authors was effective. God did guide and protect them from error—with the qualification that in the Old Testament God was moving his people progressively closer to the truth that would appear fully only in Christ. The result of inspiration is that, as the bishops at Vatican Council II stated, "the books of Scripture must be acknowledged as teaching solidly, faithfully, and without error that truth which God wanted put into sacred writings for the sake of our salvation" (*Dogmatic Constitution on Divine Revelation*, section 11). As Fr. Jerome Kodell writes, inspiration assures us that we "are in the presence of God and his truth when opening the Bible in faith" (*The Catholic Bible Study Handbook*, page 6). Despite the limitations of human words and concepts, God succeeded in conveying through Scripture exactly the truth that he wanted us to have so that we might know and love him.

While Scripture is the result of a mysterious cooperation between God and human beings, the two parties are not authors in an equal way. God is the *principal* author of the Bible. For some two thousand years, the human speakers and writers and editors took their turns composing their particular parts of the biblical material and then left the scene. But God was the author throughout—the speaker, author, and editor from beginning to end.

In order to communicate with us, God shaped his words to our capacity to hear and understand. He used human words and concepts. He accommodated himself to our limited comprehension, like a parent bending down to speak to a small child.

While God limited himself to working within the narrow range of our understanding, he allowed himself full freedom as to the types of human communication he would employ. God could and did inspire authors and editors working in a wide variety of forms—history and hymns, love songs and genealogies, letters, short stories, prophetic oracles, and others. God did not confine himself to inspiring historical narratives. Thus, just because a piece of writing is inspired does not mean that it is factual. Inspiration guarantees that it is true. But poems and fictional stories can be true in their own way—as we can see from the familiar examples of Psalm 23 ("The Lord is my shepherd...") and the parables of Jesus.

We have seen how complex were the processes by which the Bible came to be. God's inspiration was correspondingly complex. He guided those who passed on material by word of mouth. He guided each person who contributed to writing the material down, each person who shaped and rearranged it, each person who assembled it. In other words, God inspired the tradition.

Scripture not only *was* inspired; it remains inspired—"God-breathed" as the author of 2 Timothy 3:16 literally says. As we read Scripture, the God we are created to know and love meets us in his inspired word. Because the Spirit revealed God in the authors' deepest being, their words speak to us at that same

"God's word, in whatever form it comes, always has divine healing and saving power. The seven sacraments of the Church are the most vivid and direct proclamations of God's healing word in Christ. The risen Lord Jesus acts in them to extend his healing touch to the minds, hearts, and bodies of the disciples. Where conditions are right, that is, where a heart is open in faith, the seed of God's word takes root and has a sure effect. The same kind of divine power is available through God's written word in the Bible; the effect of individual readings is not as clearly defined, but the healing power of God is present. It is 'the word of God at work within you who believe' (1 Thessalonians 2:13)."
Jerome Kodell, OSB, *The Catholic Bible Study Handbook*, page 9.

level—the level where God's grace is poured into our hearts. As we read, God corrects our vision, straightens out our thinking, helps us turn away from illusions and self-delusions, opens our eyes to the light of Christ.

The Spirit that inspired the writers of Scripture became fully present in Jesus. That same Spirit now fills us as we read the Scripture that is focused on him. The Spirit reveals the Son, who is the perfect revelation of the Father. The Spirit draws us into the life of God, in which the Father loves and gives everything to the Son, and the Son loves and returns everything to the Father.

Because Scripture is God's word, we may expect God to speak to us through it. God's word is powerful, as we see in the Bible when prophets speak and, above all, when Jesus speaks (consider his words of command—Mark 1:41; 4:39; 5:41; 7:34). As God's word, the Bible is a channel of God's power. As God leads us to know him and understand his ways through Scripture, his power is at work to change us.

Because the Bible is God's word, we should come to it in humility, awe, and desire for God. But because it is also the word of human beings, we should accept the fact that it will take some effort to unearth its meanings. For the biblical books, having been composed by human beings, remain fully human. In the Bible we find God's word communicated through limited human beings. Thus we should not be surprised that it thoroughly reflects the culture and times in which the authors and editors lived. The poetry is their kind of poetry. The history is their kind of history-writing. The stories are filled with the plants and animals of *their* environment, the aspirations and conflicts of *their* society.

And yet, because the Bible brings us into contact with God, we may anticipate that the effects of reading the Bible will exceed our expectations. Scripture will confront us where we are least prepared, call us to change where we are most reluctant to try, give us comfort and hope where there is none to be seen. God gives us his Spirit so we might understand his ways and be joyful in responding to him, even in suffering. Through Scripture he calls us to live in ways that we would not have envisioned apart from his word.

Chapter Six

Whose Book Is This?

The Bible in the Church

God's life-giving revelation of himself reached its climax in the divine Word becoming flesh. Jesus revealed God in his speech and actions. He freed us from sin through his death and resurrection. He drew us into a deeply loving relationship with God by giving us his life-creating Spirit. To look at Jesus is to see God (see John 14:9).

Jesus is God's definitive, complete, final word to the human race (see Colossians 1:15-20; Hebrews 1:1-4). In Jesus, God has expressed himself to us as fully and clearly as he can. He has said all he can say. God has no further word to speak to us. Necessarily God wills that his final word should endure in the world. It is unthinkable that God would let his ultimate message to the human race die out and become lost amid the babble of human voices. He wills the revelation of himself in Jesus to continue to be available to all men and women throughout the remainder of history.

God's word is life-creating. He wishes his life-creating word to come to men and women not merely through marks of ink on paper but in a living way, so that his word might penetrate and transform our lives. God's goal in speaking his word to the world is not a book filled with words about himself but people living in union with him.

God has secured the enduring presence of his life-giving word in the world primarily in the life of a community—the group of his Son's followers, the Church. The Church is the "sign and instrument" of the saving, self-revealing work that God has accomplished through Jesus, through which human beings may be united with God and one another (*Dogmatic Constitution on the Church*, section 1). God's definitive word to the world is present in the Church's preaching and worship and in its members' lives of love, goodness, service, and self-sacrifice—lives that reflect Jesus' life, death, and resurrection. In the words and actions of Christians, all men and women should have the opportunity to encounter Jesus and, through the Church's sacramental ministry, to enter into the reconciliation with God that he has opened up through his death and resurrection.

In order for the Church to be this body of people that makes the life-giving word of Jesus available to the world, the message of Jesus must continue to be present in it with purity and power. To insure that the Church will persevere in this mission, Jesus has guaranteed his presence with it until the end of time (see Matthew 28:20). God has given the Church his Spirit, to guide it and keep it in the truth (see John 14:15-26). While all of us who are members of the Church sin and err, God protects the Church as a whole from losing the truth and holiness that he has given it in Christ.

Jesus provided for the faithfulness of his community not primarily by putting his message into writing but by authorizing a group of men to be his representatives—"apostles," that is, those who are sent. He gave them access to himself and trained them so that they would be able to live as he lived and communicate his message accurately and effectively. He prepared them to be the leadership group for his community, the foundation of its ongoing life.

The apostles carried out this commission, by the power of the Spirit. In turn they handed on this responsibility to men who came after them. As a result, the preaching of the gospel that began when Peter addressed the crowd in Jerusalem at the beginning of the Church's existence (see Acts 2) has never fallen silent. The apostolic preaching has resounded down through the centuries. God's word has continued in the Church as a living tradition, through the handing on of the teaching of Christ and the life in the Spirit from one generation to the next.

Not only the leaders but the entire Christian community share in handing on God's revelation in Christ. The tradition is embodied and communicated in the lives of Christians who study, contemplate, celebrate, and live the gospel. In the New Testament we see the whole community handing on the word of God by letting his word reshape their lives, by acting on it, by publicly acknowledging it, by presenting it to others in their ordinary circumstances (see 1 Thessalonians 1:2-10). The convert from paganism who stopped worshiping false gods, the wealthy family that opened their home to poor members of the community, the couple that adopted an abandoned infant, the man or woman who accepted death rather than deny Christ— each displayed the life of Christ, making visible the Word-made-flesh who had suffered and died for his disciples. The early Christian communities were themselves a revelation of God to the world, a revelation written not on paper or stone, but on human hearts (see 2 Corinthians 3:2-3).

The New Testament Canon

While the word of God was communicated in the living tradition of apostolic preaching and in the lives of all the members,
it was useful for the tradition to take written form. A set of writings that expressed the apostolic teaching would provide a reference point for Christian thinking and acting. As we have seen,
the early Christians did put the apostolic preaching in writing.
By about the end of the first century, the writings that later
came to be called the New Testament had come into existence.
The Gospels preserved the apostles' testimony to Jesus; Acts,
the letters, and Revelation expressed the apostolic understanding of Jesus, of the life and mission he has given us, and of the
completion of his kingdom that we may expect at the end of
time.

At the same time, there were other Christian writings in the
forms of gospels, letters, revelations. The question inevitably
arose: which writings express the genuine tradition from Jesus?
In the middle of the second century, a misguided Christian
teacher named Marcion provoked the Church to think seriously
about this question. He argued that the Church should regard
only a very small number of Christian writings as authoritative
(Luke the only Gospel, no letters but a few of Paul's). At the
same time, other Christian teachers were treating as
authoritative a much wider number of writings.

The Church gradually sifted through its earliest writings to
identify which should constitute its authoritative collection
concerning Jesus. Church leaders selected writings that were
considered to have been written by the apostles or by those who
worked with them (the author of the Gospel of Mark, for
example, was believed to have drawn his material from the

apostle Peter). The criteria were whether the writings were a genuine reflection of apostolic preaching, were in conformity with the "rule of faith" (the basic Christian convictions that became expressed in the creeds), and were in use in the Christian liturgy. In the selection process, the Spirit guided the Church to recognize which books expressed the faith that it already held and lived, the faith received from the apostles. The same Spirit that had guided writers to put the apostolic preaching about Jesus into written form guided the Church to recognize those writings that reliably conveyed that apostolic faith. Much later, Vatican Council I (1869–70) explained that the New Testament writings are the authentic expressions of the faith not because the Church says so but because it discerns that they have God as their author. The Church did not make the books of the Bible inspired; it recognized their inspiration.

By the end of the fourth century, Christians East and West had reached general agreement on the twenty-seven books that today constitute the New Testament for Catholics, Protestants, and Orthodox (although the Syrian, Egyptian, and Ethiopian branches of Christianity have slightly different New Testament collections). It was only at the Council of Trent (1545–63) that

---

"In discerning the canon of Scripture, the Church was also discerning and defining its own identity. Henceforth Scripture was to function as a mirror in which the Church could continually rediscover her identity and assess, century after century, the way in which she constantly responds to the gospel and equips herself to be an apt vehicle of its transmission."
Pontifical Biblical Commission, *The Interpretation of the Bible in the Church*, page 144.

an ecumenical council formally defined these twenty-seven books as constituting the New Testament canon, but Trent was simply affirming what had been established for more than a thousand years.

The term "canon" comes from a Semitic word for reed, or measuring rod. Applied to Scripture, canon means that this collection of books is considered to be inspired by God in such a way as to serve as the regulating rule for faith and moral teaching. (Here we have been examining the formation of the New Testament. On the Church's definition of the Old Testament canon, see the accompanying box on the differences between the Catholic and Protestant Bibles.)

Why Are the Catholic and the Protestant Bibles Different?

Before the Church produced and acknowledged the writings that constitute the New Testament, it received the writings that constitute the Old Testament. By the time of Jesus and the apostles, some writings had become recognized among Jews as Scripture. Jesus used and interpreted these writings as Scripture, and the early Church accepted them.

Questions inevitably arose, however, because the body of authoritative writings was not defined for Jews in the time of Jesus. Jews in Palestine used a smaller collection of books as Scripture, while Greek-speaking Jews outside Palestine used a larger collection (this collection was in Greek and is called the Septuagint—from the Greek word for seventy, since it was said to have been produced by seventy translators). In addition, the larger collection, at least, seems not to have been strictly defined. Which collection should the Church regard as its Old Testament?

Since Christianity spread predominantly within the Roman empire, where Greek was the international language, Christians in the first three centuries widely used the larger collection. In the fourth century, some Christian teachers, such as St. Athanasius and St. Jerome, thought the Church should limit its Old Testament to the shorter list of books that had been used by Jews in Palestine—and which, by the second century, had established itself as the official Bible of Jews everywhere. Others, such as St. Augustine, maintained that the larger set of books should be maintained as the Church's Old Testament, on the basis of its long-standing use. Sirach, for example, which belonged only to the larger collection, was very widely used in the early Church.

Why Jewish leaders had settled on the shorter set is not entirely clear. It may have had something to do with language: the shorter set of books were in Hebrew and Aramaic, while some of the additional books in the longer set were written in Greek. But language does not entirely account for the Jewish decision to embrace the shorter set, since some of the additional works had been composed in Hebrew or Aramaic (Sirach, 1 Maccabees, Tobit). In any case, by the fifth century the Church both East and West generally settled on the longer collection as its Old Testament (although East Syrian, Egyptian, and Ethiopian Christians recognize a slightly different set of Old Testament books).

In the sixteenth century, however, the Protestant Reformers returned to the shorter collection. They did this partly from a desire to exclude 2 Maccabees, which was used by Catholics to defend the doctrine of purgatory, which Protestants rejected (see 2 Maccabees 12:42-46). The Reformers may also have wished to return to the Scripture that Jesus used. (In the sixteenth century, scholars were not aware that the larger collection of books was widely recognized by Jews in Jesus' time.)

In response to the Reformers, the Council of Trent in 1546 gave official Catholic recognition to the longer collection of books, as found in the ancient Latin translation of St. Jerome (called the "Vulgate," or "ordinary language," Latin translation).

Living Tradition

We have seen that God guided the oral traditions that lie behind the Old and New Testaments and that he guided the authors and editors at every step as they composed and refined the texts through the many stages of development. But God's guiding presence with his people did not decrease as the volumes accumulated on the biblical library shelves. Jesus is Emmanuel—"God with us" (Matthew 1:23). Through the incarnation of his Word and the gift of his Spirit, God has irreversibly established his presence among us.

The Spirit's guidance now produces no new Scripture but leads us to deeper understanding and new applications of God's revelation in Christ. God's Spirit enlivens the handing on of the revelation of Jesus Christ in every age of the Church. By the Spirit it is a living tradition—the tradition of a community that experiences the life that it speaks about. Only a living tradition could transmit the revelation of the living God.

In order to understand the place of the Bible in this living tradition, it is helpful to distinguish two senses in which the word "tradition" is used. There is tradition in the sense of content—"that which is handed on." There is also "tradition" in the sense of process—the "handing on."

The Bible is the written form of "that which is handed on" from Christ to the apostles and from the apostles to every later generation. Scripture is not the only part of "that which is handed on." The authoritative tradition of the Church has been handed on in other forms also. The Church has handed on its creeds (summary expressions of its faith) and its liturgy (the basic structure of its worship), for these, too, reflect the Church's Spirit-guided understanding of Christ and of itself.

The "handing on" occurs in the bishops' preaching and teaching, in the celebration of the Eucharist and the sacraments, in the professing of the creed, and in Christians' testimony to Jesus through lives of holiness and compassionate service.

"What was handed on by the Apostles includes everything which contributes toward the holiness of life and increase in faith of the people of God; and so the Church, in her teaching, life, and worship, perpetuates and hands on to all generations all that she herself is, all that she believes." *Dogmatic Constitution on Divine Revelation*, section 8.

Obviously "that which is handed on" and the "handing on" are inseparable. The Scriptures are the written part of the tradition of the community which God has entrusted with the task of making the gospel known. While the Bible is open to anyone who wishes to read it, it belongs to the Church in a way similar to the way in which the Declaration of Independence and the Constitution belong to the people of the United States.

Since Scripture is the written form of the tradition of a community, it is only within that community that it can be properly understood. The Bible is the book of the Church; the Church is its home, the place where a living tradition provides the keys for unlocking its meaning. The central purpose of the Bible is to lead us to know, love, and serve God, and we attain this purpose by entering into the knowledge of God that is already present in the Church. If we do not have some experience of the forgiveness, mercy, humility, power, and glory of God from the life and worship of the Church, we will not be able to grasp these realities when we find them spoken of in the pages of the Bible. The authors of Scripture received their inspiration not as independent operators but as members of God's people. Correspondingly, God inspires us to understand the Bible as we participate in the life of his people. We get in touch with Jesus Christ through the Church, which is his body (see 1 Corinthians 12:27).

We can see the importance of reading the Bible in the Church by asking, "When we read the Bible, how can we be sure we will hear God's word, not merely our own—or other people's—ideas buzzing around inside our heads?" Concern for authentic interpretation of the Christian tradition was already an issue in the early Christian community (see 2 Peter 3:15-16) and will always remain. The Bible is not completely self-interpreting; no written document ever is. We interpret every piece of writing within some frame of reference. The question is, "What will our interpretive framework be?" To be truly understood, Scripture must be explored in the context of the faith in which it was written. That means reading each part within the whole canon which the Church has assembled, and reading the whole canon within the tradition of the Church's teaching, life, and worship. Only in this way can we know that we are interpreting Scripture in the Spirit in which it was written.

To some people, it may seem confining to accept the Church as the normative context in which to read Scripture. They would prefer a more neutral location from which to read. But there is no such neutral location. We all bring presuppositions with us to the reading of the Bible. None of us is a blank slate. We are all creatures of our culture, in ways that we never entirely perceive. As Jerome Kodell puts it, if we do not take the Church as our authoritative guide to Scripture, we expose ourselves "to the danger of following, without realizing it, an unidentified authority." This might be "prejudice, materialism, or American common sense" (*The Catholic Bible Study Handbook*, page 17).

"There are two stages in the relationship between the Bible and Tradition. For the birth and growth of revelation, it was the Spirit's role to act on the living Tradition in such a way that it was gradually crystallized into Scripture. When revelation was complete in its written form, it was the Spirit's role to interpret it and continue to give it life by Tradition." Celestin Charlier, *The Christian Approach to the Bible*, page 236.

At points in our reading of the Bible, we need authoritative clarification. Were Jesus' "brothers" also children of his mother Mary (see Mark 6:3)? In what way is Jesus present in the Eucharist (see Matthew 26:26-28)? In the history of the Church such questions have given rise to considerable debate, because there has seemed to be more than one way to interpret what Scripture says. It is a great blessing that Jesus commissioned his apostles to teach in his name (see Mark 3:13-19; Matthew 16:17-19). With the guidance of the Spirit, the apostles and their designated successors, the pope and bishops, have been able to provide definitive answers to such questions.

In doing so, popes and bishops have not added to the revelation given once and for all in Christ. Rather they have given authentic—authorized—interpretations of that revelation. The bishops do not stand "over" Scripture as judges. "This teaching office is not superior to the Word of God," the bishops declared at Vatican Council II (*Dogmatic Constitution on Divine Revelation*, section 10). The Bible functions as the canon, the standard for the Church. But who is to apply the standard to the Church? The Church needs an authorized body of leaders to give an authentic application of the standard. That is the office of the bishops, the successors of the apostles. The bishops' authority to teach is referred to by the term "magisterium"—teaching office. As George Martin has pointed out, it makes no sense to accept the canon of Scripture defined by an authoritative Church leadership in the past, yet reject the same authoritative Church leadership in the present when it interprets the contents of that canon. "To do so would be to claim that the Holy Spirit who guided the early Church no longer guides the Church in our time" (*Reading Scripture As the Word of God*, page 156).

It is, however, important not to exaggerate the extent to which the pope and bishops have given authoritative interpretations of Scripture. As Pope Pius XII observed in 1943, the instances are rather few (*Divino Afflante Spiritu*). The magisterium does not tell us what everything in the Bible means. Even when the magisterium speaks authoritatively about something in the Bible, it usually does not attempt to provide an exhaustive interpretation. Sometimes it rules that a certain interpretation of a passage is mistaken, as in its judgment that the thousand-year reign of Christ in Revelation 20 is not to be interpreted as an earthly event. Sometimes the Church grounds a portion of its teaching in a specific passage of the Bible—as when it connects the sacrament of reconciliation with 1 John 1:5-2:2 and the sacrament of anointing with James 5:14-15. But these declarations do not attempt to expound the entire meaning of the passages in question.

In one sense, Scripture is complete. It is the Church's canon, the complete yardstick for measuring its teaching. No further writings can be added to it. But the Bible is not the complete book of theology, the complete book of liturgy, the complete hymnbook, the complete guide to evangelism or marriage or fundraising. Not everything that we need to know for Christian faith and life is contained in Scripture in the form in which we need it. The Bible is the norm for all later teaching, liturgy, sacraments. It is the "soul" of theology (*Dogmatic Constitution on Divine Revelation*, section 24). But the Bible does not contain the entire tradition of the Church.

The Bible does not answer all the questions we encounter about Christian life. What are the appropriate forms for Christian prayer and community worship? How does one apply Jesus' teaching about material possessions, about living as a servant of others, about trusting God? What does it mean to be guided by the Spirit? At many such points in our reading, we need clarification and guidance about application.

Isn't the Bible Self-Interpreting?

Many evangelical and fundamentalist Protestants insist that the Bible is self-interpreting and thus there is no need for a magisterium to provide authoritative interpretation. Indeed, they see this principle as important for establishing the authority of God's word, which might otherwise seem to fall under the authority of human interpreters.

But numerous interpretive issues arise in reading the Bible. Which things are to be taken as straightforward statements, which are to be taken as metaphors and symbols? How do the various parts of the Bible fit together? In what ways does the Old Testament speak about Christ, the Church, and Christian life? How are the prophecies of Scripture to be applied to society today, to Judaism, to the Church?

When such questions arise, it becomes clear that all readers depend on some interpretive tradition. No reader develops an absolutely independent interpretation of the Bible. In practice, readers look for guidance to help solve problems. This is an eminently sensible thing to do. The question is, to whom shall we look for guidance? To answer interpretive questions, many evangelical and fundamentalist Christians rely on Bible teachers or prophecy experts, rather than on the tradition and teaching office of the Church or contemporary biblical scholarship.

Evangelical and fundamentalist reliance on prophecy experts, for example, is clearly demonstrated in the great popularity of these experts' elaborate schemes which fit together parts of the Bible to produce scenarios for the end of world history. These scenarios are not found in the Bible but are constructed by correlating widely separated statements in Daniel, Revelation, and other biblical books. At every step in the construction, biblical statements are given interpretations that are far from obvious. The result is not submission to the Bible but submission of the Bible to one or another scheme of interpretation. The schemes of interpretation vary, according to the preferences and personality of their originators.

This is not to say, of course, that people who do not accept the Church as the authoritative interpreter of Scripture may not be earnest about submitting their lives to God's word. Many evangelicals and fundamentalists set a high example in applying Scripture to their lives and following Christ in authentic discipleship.

Thus we need to read the Bible in relation to the larger tradition of which it is part, for the tradition supplements it and aids us in applying it to our lives. To live a life that truly reflects the purposes of God, we need more than the Bible; we need the wisdom of the Church's living tradition—the traditions of prayer and liturgy and sacramental celebration and the lives and writings of the saints. These traditions are hardly monolithic. The gospel has been appropriated in countless ways in different cultures and ages. To be guided by these traditions in shaping our Christian lives does not mean walking a narrow path but swimming in a broad river.

In practice, the local Christian communities of diocese and parish, pastored by our bishop and priest, are the natural places for growing in our understanding of Scripture. Here we should be reading Scripture with others, discussing it, listening to one another. Our pastors are gifted to guide us in our reflection on Scripture so that we might hear what the Spirit is saying in our hearts and learn to respond. In the parish setting also we have the opportunity to listen to those whose grasp of Scripture may be simpler but deeply lived. Sometimes the poorest, neediest members of the Christian community, because they rely most heavily on God's help, are able to hear and apply his word in a particularly acute way (see James 2:5).

Chapter Seven

How Do We Know What It Means?
Interpreting the Bible

In the Bible, as in Jesus, the divine and the human combine. Pope Pius XII wrote that "just as the Word of God became like men in every respect except sin, so too the words of God, expressed in human languages, became like human language in every respect except error" (*Divino Afflante Spiritu*). In Jesus, there is no dividing line between the divine and the human. Everything he did on earth was at once a human action and an act of God. In Scripture there is no division between what God wrote and what human beings wrote. God inspired the human authors, with the result that what they said is what God said.

As we have seen, the human beings who wrote the biblical books acted as real, thinking authors and editors. Since God did not bypass their minds when he inspired them to write, we cannot bypass their meanings if we wish to learn what he has to say to us through their words. "Seeing that, in sacred Scripture,

---

"To compose the sacred books, God chose certain men who, all the while he employed them in this task, made full use of their powers and faculties so that, though he acted in them and by them, it was as true authors that they consigned to writing whatever he wanted written, and no more." *Dogmatic Constitution on Divine Revelation*, section 11.

God speaks through men in human fashion, it follows that the interpreter of sacred Scriptures, if he is to ascertain what God wished to communicate to us, should carefully search out the meaning which the sacred writers really had in mind, that meaning which God had thought well to manifest through the medium of their words" *(Dogmatic Constitution on Divine Revelation,* section 12). God expressed himself through the human authors. We can discover his meaning only by discovering the meanings that those authors and editors expressed. St. Augustine wrote, "To understand the divine oracles properly, there must be a constant effort to reach the mind of the author. It is through him that the Holy Spirit has spoken" (quoted by Celestin Charlier, *The Christian Approach to the Bible,* page 33). This principle is the starting point for all interpretation of Scripture.

The Literal Meaning

Biblical interpretation searches out the meaning that the authors and editors expressed. In investigating the meaning of Scripture we do not delve into the hidden recesses of the authors' minds and speculate about what they might have intended but failed to communicate. We seek the meaning they embodied in their words. To put it another way, we try to grasp the meaning their words would have had for their first readers.

In contemporary Catholic usage, this "meaning that the authors and editors expressed" is called the *literal* meaning. The literal meaning is simply what the authors and editors meant by their words. Using this definition, the literal meaning of a metaphorical text is whatever the author meant by the metaphor. The literal meaning of "the Lord is my shepherd" (Psalm 23:1) is not "God raises sheep, and I am one," but "God cares for me in every way." When Jesus said that if your hand leads you into sin you should cut it off (see Matthew 5:30), his literal meaning was not "amputate your hand" but "take radical measures to resist temptation." The other interpretations ("God raises sheep," "chop off your hand") might be called "literalistic," rather than "literal."

In most cases we should speak about Scripture's *literal* meanings, in the plural. We all know how complex human communication can be. Even a straightforward, everyday piece of writing may have more than one level of meaning. Consider, for example, a simple e-mail from my boss telling me to fly to Houston to close a deal. My boss's choice of words may imply how important she thinks the deal is. The fact that she is sending the e-mail to me rather than to someone else in the office may suggest that she has confidence in me even though my last trip was unsuccessful. Her sending me out of town at this time may be a reminder that she's the boss, even though I have been complaining about too much traveling.

If a business e-mail may have layers of meaning, the same is certainly true of the Bible. In fact, the biblical writers and editors often pack meanings rather densely into their texts. Density of meaning is typical of poetry, of which there is a great deal in the Bible; it also characterizes the Bible's prose sections. Some biblical authors, such as the apostle John who wrote the richly symbolic book of Revelation, created numerous levels of meaning by alluding to many other biblical passages.

From the Literal to the Spiritual Meaning

A person's writing expresses his or her conscious intention. It is possible, however, for the full meaning of what someone writes to exceed what the writer consciously intended. Other people may discover more meaning in the written words than the writer realized. Readers may notice unsuspected implications; they may draw out new applications. Owners of African-American slaves were among the group of American colonists in 1776, who wrote that "all men are created equal" and are "endowed by their Creator" with "liberty." A few decades later, other Americans came to see in these statements a charter of freedom for the slaves. The abolitionists were not changing the meaning of the Declaration of Independence. Rather, they were more sensitive to the document's meaning than some of its authors had been. They grasped, as the authors had not, that the universality of the Declaration ("*all* men are created equal") removes any justification for slave-holding. It was the literal meaning—the *authors'* meaning—not an alien meaning, that the abolitionists saw in the document.

Something like this happened in the process of the Bible's formation. In some cases, biblical authors expressed hopes and ideals that were later seen to point toward fulfillments greater than the authors had realized. For example, psalmists composed acclamations for the Israelite kings that expressed an idealized vision of kingship (see Psalms 2, 45). These psalms pointed toward a reign that no earthly king could accomplish—toward God's perfect kingship over the earth. The psalmists who wrote the royal psalms might have been astonished at the way God fulfilled their aspirations for his kingdom on earth through Jesus. Yet the kingdom that Jesus inaugurated, which will ultimately bring complete peace and well-being to human beings under God's loving rule, is an extension of the psalmists' meaning.

Sometimes later events give a document greater significance. In the future, I may look back on this week's e-mail as a harbinger of a period when I began to travel excessively. If the deal succeeds, the e-mail may stand as evidence for my boss's growing shrewdness as a negotiator. These meanings would not have been present in her mind when she wrote, but her e-mail could acquire these further meanings without losing or reversing its original meaning. In fact, these larger meanings would build on its earlier meaning—that she wanted me to go to Houston.

A similar growth in significance occurred in the biblical tradition. For example, as God unfolded his plans in history, his earlier actions became the models of later actions. Thus the earlier events acquired a significance that their original narrators did not conceive of. The story of the exodus from Egypt later spoke to the Jewish exiles in Babylon as an assurance that God would bring them release also (see how the themes of Exodus 15:1-18 are taken up in Isaiah 43:16-19). This is not to say that those who originally handed on the exodus story had any notion of speaking about a Babylonian exile, which lay centuries in the future. Yet readers during the exile found this message of hope in the exodus. And they truly *found* this meaning in the exodus story, rather than imposing this meaning on it, for the exodus from Egypt demonstrated God's love and faithfulness toward Israel, and that same God was with the exiles in Babylon, unfolding a plan that would lead them through a similar passage to freedom.

As discussed in chapter three, portions of biblical books acquired new meanings as they were assembled with other portions. The accounts of Abraham and Sarah began as family stories giving assurance of God's presence to them and their descendants. When these accounts (Genesis 12–25) were combined with the earlier chapters about creation and human rebellion against God (Genesis 1–11), it became apparent that God's dealings with Abraham and Sarah were part of a larger plan. Against the background of the earlier stories, God's call to Abraham and Sarah appears as a step toward remedying the alienation that had opened up between himself and the human race. This meaning was an enlargement, not a reversal, of the original Abraham and Sarah traditions.

The process of discerning meanings in the biblical texts reached its climax in Jesus. He understood the meaning of the Scripture that preceded him more clearly than anyone else because he perceived with perfect clarity the goals toward which God had been working throughout history. He went to the heart of the biblical tradition in his preaching of utter dependence on God as heavenly Father and of love of neighbor even to the point of laying down one's life.

Jesus presented himself not only as the supreme interpreter but as the personal fulfillment of the expectations that God's words and deeds had aroused in the history of Israel (see Luke 24:27). But Jesus gave an unexpected fulfillment. In Jesus' teaching, as reflected in the New Testament writings, God's intentions for his people were transposed into a new key. God's liberation of Israel from slavery in Egypt was interpreted as a foretaste of a greater rescue of men and women from sin and death (see Exodus 12; 1 Corinthians 5:7). God's promises to destroy the enemies of his people and reestablish the kingdom of Israel (see Daniel 7) were seen to point toward the end of the devil's dominion over human lives and the coming of the Spirit (see John 12:31; Acts 1:3-8). The atonement accomplished through the sacrifices in the Jerusalem temple (Leviticus 16) was interpreted as a prefigurement of the perfect atonement that would overcome the distance between God and human beings and make a profound interior change in us (see Hebrews 5; 7–10). The Old Testament expectation of a regathered Israel worshiping God in a more glorious Jerusalem temple (see Ezekiel 40–47) was seen as an image of the community of Jesus' followers gathered into eternal life with him (see Revelation 4–5; 21).

Although Jesus' interpretation of the Old Testament writings went far beyond what the original authors and editors conceived, Jesus claimed not to be changing the meaning of the biblical writings but to be bringing their true meaning to light. He saw himself as completing the plan of God that those writings spoke about. The biblical books, Jesus declared, had pointed to him all along (see John 5:39-46).

In Christian tradition, this level of meaning in the Bible— the level on which it speaks about Christ and life in him—is called the *spiritual* meaning. In the Old Testament writings, the authors and editors probably did not perceive how their writings pointed toward Christ. The spiritual meaning was not part of their conscious intention but was a higher or deeper meaning of their words. We might say that it is the meaning of the Old Testament seen from God's angle of vision. In the New Testament, where the authors did explicitly intend to speak about Christ, the spiritual meaning of their words is the same as the meaning that was consciously present in their minds as they wrote.

Despite the unexpectedness of the spiritual meaning of the Old Testament, it is truly part of the meaning of the Old Testament. The spiritual meaning is an extension or deepening of the literal meaning, never a reversal of it. The events narrated in the Old Testament—such as God's covenant with Abraham, the exodus from Egypt, Israel's possession of the land of Canaan—belonged to the one stream of divine activity that was heading toward the coming of Jesus. God was

---

Levels of Meaning

The layers of meaning in the Bible may be distinguished as literal and spiritual. The literal meaning is that intended by the authors as expressed in their words. The spiritual is that which points to Christ in ways that extend or deepen the literal meaning. Sometimes the spiritual meaning of an Old Testament text is called the "sensus plenior," Latin for "fuller sense." Traditionally, the spiritual meaning has been subdivided into three levels: (1) the "typological," or "allegorical," by which realities and events in the Old Testament function as signs of Christ and sacramental life; (2) the "moral," or "tropological," by which the persons and events offer lessons about how we should live; and (3) the "anagogical," (meaning "leading upward"), by which realities and events stand as images of our final fulfillment in Christ (for example, the city of Jerusalem represents the gathering of God's people in the new creation). For these levels of meaning, and other explanations for how Scripture communicates its message, see the *Catechism of the Catholic Church*, sections 101-33.

preparing for and prefiguring the coming of his Son. Since there was a connection in the events, there is a connection in the writings that recounted the events. The spiritual meaning grows out of the literal meaning as flower from seed.

Discovering the Literal Meaning

How do we draw out the literal and spiritual meanings of Scripture? To understand the literal meaning of Scripture, we need to pay attention to several factors:

1. Type of writing. To understand what you read—or hear or view—you have to know what *kind* of communication you are receiving. You would reach ludicrous and dangerous conclusions if you took the computer-generated fantasies of a car commercial as a guide for how to drive (it's not a training video) or made decisions about cancer treatment from what you saw in a TV soap opera about doctors (it's not a documentary). The biblical library contains various types of writing (in discussions of the Bible sometimes called "genres"), and we must distinguish them if we are to understand them. A poem "means" differently from a letter, a parable differently from a history.

Since the Bible was composed in cultural settings quite different from ours, some of its types of writing are unfamiliar to us. Mythological tales, tribal traditions, prophecies—these types of writing are generally not part of our modern Western culture. They may be as puzzling to us as a car commercial would be to a person who lived in the time of Christ. The biblical library also contains types of writing that are familiar to us—memoirs, genealogies, essays—but often in forms different from ours.

Learning how the different kinds of biblical writings "work" is crucial for understanding what the authors and editors were saying. For example, the starting point for understanding the references to dominion in Psalm 2 is to recognize that it celebrates the enthronement of an Israelite king. Knowing that Exodus 20:1–24:8 is an adaptation of an ancient covenant formula helps us discover the main points and not get lost in the mass of legal details.

Awareness of the types of material in the Bible steers us clear of misunderstanding. Familiarity with the nature of apocalyptic writing will protect us from the temptation to strip-mine the books of Daniel or Revelation for references to specific twenty-first-century events. We will be less appalled at the bloody ending of the book of Esther if we know that the book is fiction.

2. Background. Is a dollar tip generous or stingy? Is a question about a person's ethnic identity a discriminatory act? Obviously it all depends. To answer these questions you have to know whether the tip-leaver just ate a piece of pie or a five-course meal, whether the questioner is a census-taker or a potential employer. In addition to such immediate context, or foreground information, you need to know background information. In what situations is tipping normal and how much is expected? Why might a census-taker or an employer want to know about a person's ethnicity?

Writers regularly supply the first—"foreground"—type of information. But they often count on their readers being familiar with the background and say little about it. This presents a problem when writer and reader come from different cultures. If the writer has assumed that the reader knows about etiquette, monetary values, patterns of courtship, religious ceremonies, business practices, and so on, the reader unfamiliar with such background will have a hard time following the story. This, of course, is often our situation reading the Bible.

It is difficult to understand Abraham's behavior when he and Sarah take refuge in Egypt (see Genesis 12:10-20) unless we know something about the vulnerability of pastoral people in their dealings with city people. The reader cannot grasp the drama of the confrontation between Judah and Assyria (see 2 Kings 18–19) without knowing a little about the behavior of Assyrian armies (horrendous!). Why is it so significant that Ruth comes from Moab (see Ruth 1:1-4)? Why does Jesus so sternly instruct his followers not to tell anyone that he is the Messiah (see Mark 8:29-30)? And what does "Messiah" mean? We need background!

In many cases we will miss the full meaning of a passage unless we view it against its cultural background. For example, ancient Near Eastern peoples conceived of creation as the outcome of a struggle between gods. In Mesopotamian stories, the sea was pictured as a divine ocean-monster who was vanquished and divided up to form the world. In Genesis 1, by contrast, God creates not by conflict but simply by command. The sea is merely part of God's creation; sea beasts are elements of the ecosystem, not divine powers. Thus the biblical message is that

---

"We need to understand the biblical authors' languages, the things they assumed as they spoke to other people in their cultures, the usual ways that people communicated with each other in those cultures." Pope Pius XII, *Divino Afflante Spiritu.*

God holds absolute sovereignty and exercises limitless creative power. This message emerges clearly only when we compare the Genesis account to the creation stories of Israel's polytheistic neighbors.

Often what speakers and writers do not say is as important as what they do say. But only someone familiar with the culture will be able to "hear" the silences. In many psalms people ask God for healing (see Psalms 6, 22, 31). To some extent, these prayers resemble the prayers of the Israelites' pagan neighbors to their various gods. But the Israelites' psalms are missing something in their neighbors' prayers: the psalms contain no incantations against evil spirits. The Israelites shared their neighbors' belief that evil spirits can inflict sicknesses, but they did not use magic to drive them out. Rather, they simply asked God for healing. The absence of incantations expressed the Israelites' trust in God's mercy, faithfulness, and power.

Just as ignorance of types of writing can lead to serious misunderstandings, so can ignorance of background. The author of the Gospel of John often calls Jesus' opponents "the Jews" (John 5:15-18; 7:1; 9:18). The reader who does not understand the first-century religious situation may mistakenly think that John is condemning Judaism or venting anti-Semitism. In fact, all the characters in these incidents are Jewish, both those who reject Jesus and those who accept him, and the author himself is Jewish. But, against the background of conflict between Christians and Jews in the latter part of the first century, the author often uses the term "Jews" to refer to Jewish religious authorities who opposed Jesus.

3. Purpose and situation. Hosea prophesied, "I desire steadfast love and not sacrifice" (Hosea 6:6). Was that a declaration that God wanted the Jewish sacrificial system dismantled? Paul criticized the Christians in Galatia for wanting to observe "special days, and months, and seasons" (Galatians 4:10). Was he ruling out an annual liturgical cycle? You might think so, if you did not understand the purposes of their statements. Both Hosea and Paul were combating distorted views of how people should relate to God. Their words were verbal attacks. But an attack does not provide a well-rounded treatment of a subject. When we recognize Hosea's and Paul's purposes, we will not try to find in their words comprehensive statements about how the various aspects of religious practice should fit together.

Since the prophets constantly addressed particular social and political situations, extensive sections of the prophetic books become comprehensible—and interesting—only when we have some idea of the situations they were dealing with. Many of the New Testament letters were written to counter false understandings of the gospel. Failing to consider what those false views were, some commentators have arrived at flawed interpretations. Commenting on a text by St. Paul, St. Athanasius, a great Christian teacher in the fourth century, wrote: "Here, as in all passages of Scripture, we must observe the occasion of the apostle's utterance and note carefully and accurately the person and the subject which were the cause of his writing. Ignorance or error concerning these points can lead us to misconceive the meaning of the author" (quoted by Celestin Charlier, *The Christian Approach to the Bible*, page 34).

A case in point is Paul's words in his letter to the Galatians criticizing "works of the law" (3:10). Paul was rejecting the view of some Christian missionaries that gentile Christians must become Jews and undertake to follow the entire Mosaic law. By dismissing "works of the law," Paul was not indiscriminately criticizing all religious practices, but rejecting an emphasis on certain ceremonial aspects of Old Testament legislation. He was certainly not asserting that our own cooperation with God's grace plays no part in our salvation. But Paul's words against "works of the law" have sometimes been misunderstood and misapplied as an argument against the Catholic sacramental system and the Catholic emphasis on the importance of our human cooperation with God's grace.

4. Structure. The books of the Bible were painstakingly written and edited. This is not to say there are no rough edges and "seams," where sections have been joined, or that everything in the Bible rises to the level of great literature. But the care, and even artistry, with which the books of Scripture are composed invite close attention to their form and manner of expression. Appreciation of the biblical books as literature is a doorway to understanding.

Ancient writers, however, fashioned their works in patterns unfamiliar to us. Without some sense of how ancient writers composed their poems and ordered their historical narratives, we will miss some of the artistry—and thus some of the meaning. For example, ancient Semitic writers were fond of bringing a section of writing to an end by returning to an idea or word used at the beginning (thus creating an "inclusion"). This provided a sense of closure and had the practical benefit of marking off a section (in those days books did not have chapter divisions or subheadings). Noticing this pattern helps us see how the writers divided their material into units, and this, in turn, helps us follow their train of thought. To take another example, letters in the ancient Greek-speaking world usually followed common patterns of introduction, body, and conclusion. Recognizing this structure in a New Testament letter may be helpful for identifying the writer's central concern.

The Help We Need

The practical conclusion from these considerations is quite simple. We need the help of scholars in order to discover the biblical authors' meanings.

We need, first of all, the kind of help that biblical scholars call "historical-critical" ("critical" here does not mean having a negative attitude but proceeding according to defined methods and criteria of investigation). Historical-critical method explores the history that lies behind the biblical books—the oral traditions, the formation of written documents, how documents were used as sources in composing the books, how later editors revised and assembled the material, and the historical situations that the biblical writers were dealing with. Scholars working along these lines draw on studies into ancient languages and literature, information about ancient cultures and events derived from archaeology and ancient writings, anthropological and sociological studies, and other kinds of research. These kinds of expertise aid our understanding of the human authors' meaning—which is the primary point where we make contact with God's message for us. This is why, from Pope Pius XII in the 1940s to Pope John Paul II in the 1990s, the Church has made it clear that such scholarly help is indispensable for understanding the Bible.

While some scholars contribute to our understanding of the biblical books by examining the history behind and around them, others help us understand the biblical books as finished writings. This work is sometimes called "literary criticism." Having become familiar with the literature of the ancient world, these scholars can help us understand how the writings of the Bible are structured and the artistry by which they achieved their purposes to instruct and encourage.

While scholarly help is necessary for understanding Scripture, it must be acknowledged that there have been problems with modern biblical scholarship. The Pontifical Biblical Commission, an advisory body of Catholic scholars selected by the Holy See, pointed out several deficiencies in a 1993 document entitled *The Interpretation of the Bible in the Church*:

- Scholars sometimes treat Scripture as though it were merely an ancient document, part of a world that has passed away. The Bible then seems separated from the present by an unbridgeable gulf of centuries.
- Historical methods which illuminate the stages of writing and editing of the Bible bring out the human side of the text—but with the danger that the reader will lose sight of the fact that these human words are also the word of God.
- Scholarly methods that dissect the biblical writings into their sources may seem to leave Scripture in pieces. The sense of a whole, of a unified message, may be lost.
- In an effort to be impartial, some scholars may set faith to one side. But Scripture calls us to commitment to God. To read it in a detached way, not hearing or responding to that call, is to fail to penetrate its central meaning for us.
- The tools of scholarly study, which are of themselves neutral, may be employed to achieve partisan agendas. Scholarship has sometimes been used to attack the Church by attempting to demonstrate that the biblical writings on which the Church bases its faith and practice are forgeries, falsehoods,

not the work of the apostles, and so on. Theories about the development of the early Church have been used to dismiss some of the biblical writings as historically unreliable. At times, a rationalistic mind-set has written off miracle stories as inventions.

The Church has needed to defend the faith against problems such as these. The late-nineteenth-century pontiff Leo XIII encouraged Catholic biblical scholarship mainly as a defense against such problems. The Church has been concerned that Catholic scholars not import into their work views that are alien to the Christian tradition; for example, that miracles must be attributable to merely natural causes or that Jesus did not intend to establish a Church.

But the popes have also defended modern biblical scholarship for its inherent value for the Church. In a statement in 1993, John Paul II pointed out that preceding popes "vehemently" encouraged modern biblical studies. Citing Pius XII, John Paul noted that modern methods of scholarship are useful not only for responding to outside attacks on the Church's understanding of Scripture, but also for the Church's own study of Scripture. The Church does not use modern scholarship on the outside while relying inside on more "spiritual" methods. Rather, he declared, the historical-critical method, freed from philosophical presuppositions contrary to truth and faith, is the starting point for understanding Scripture, since it is the starting point for grasping the human authors' meanings (in Pontifical Biblical Commission, *The Interpretation of the Bible in the Church*).

In the last century, some Catholics have wanted to abandon or ignore modern biblical scholarship and return instead to the interpretations of the Church Fathers of the first Christian centuries, such as St. John Chrysostom and St. Augustine. Certainly we should read the Fathers' homilies and commentaries on Scripture. They sought Christ in all the pages of the Old Testament, desiring personal encounter with him—which makes them a model for how to read the Bible. The Fathers' comments on Scripture are marked by depth, sensitivity, hunger for God, appreciation of the mystery of Christ.

Nevertheless, the Fathers' interpretive approach has weaknesses as well as strengths. The Fathers had little sense of the human authors as authors, of their world, of the historical development of revelation. They mainly viewed the Bible as simply authored by God. The modern focus on history and on the human dimension of the biblical books enriches rather than diminishes the reading of Scripture. The exploration of the texts from a human point of view can lead to a deepening of our understanding of what God was doing and what he wished to communicate to us. Modern linguistic, historical, cultural, and literary tools help us grasp the multilayered meanings of Scripture, helping us see how traditions developed and what the various parts of Scripture meant at the times in which they were written and edited. Seeing how God dealt with people in their particular circumstances and cultures helps us see how he may wish to deal with us today.

The Fathers did not regard themselves as having spoken the last interpretive words on the Bible. They were very much aware of unfathomed depths in Scripture. That later scholars might shed new light on the Bible would not have surprised them at all. It is not uncommon for St. Jerome or St. Augustine, for example, to offer various opinions about a single passage, express puzzlement, and declare their openness to someone offering a better interpretation.

In the last couple of centuries, scholars working in various fields have learned an enormous amount about the ancient Near Eastern and Mediterranean worlds where the Bible was written. This is not to say that Christians and Jews in the past could not understand the Bible. But aspects of the Bible have become accessible in new ways. As the Pontifical Biblical Commission declared, modern studies have "made it possible to understand far more accurately the intention of the authors and editors of the Bible, as well as the message which they addressed to their first readers" (*The Interpretation of the Bible in the Church*). In the pursuit of the truth communicated to us in Scripture, it would be wrong to ignore these tools for understanding. To do so would not be safer; it would be anti-intellectual. Quoting Leo XIII, in the statement mentioned above Pope John Paul II encouraged biblical scholars to "be alert to adopt without delay anything useful that each period brings to biblical exegesis." In *Divino Afflante Spiritu*, Pius XII reminded those who regarded modern biblical scholarship as a threat that "not everything new is to be feared"!

On balance, we need both newer and older approaches to the Bible. The historical-critical method is necessary, but not enough by itself. The same is true of the interpretations of the

---

"The sacred Synod encourages those sons of the Church who are engaged in biblical studies constantly to renew their efforts, in order to carry on the work they have so happily begun, with complete dedication and in accordance with the mind of the Church." *Dogmatic Constitution on Divine Revelation*, section 23.

Fathers and other writers of the past. To plumb the depths of Scripture, we need both the Fathers and modern scholars. The wise person draws from the old and the new (see Matthew 13:52).

Discovering the Spiritual Meaning

Christ is the center of God's saving action toward us, the light who illuminates God's whole plan of salvation. The various parts of the Bible yield their true meaning when read by his light. Thus we read the Bible for its spiritual meaning, the Old Testament in reference to the New.

In a famous line, St. Augustine wrote that the New Testament is concealed in the Old, the Old Testament is made manifest in the New. While the spiritual meaning of the Old Testament is not contrary to the literal meaning, it is hidden, because it concerns God's plan of salvation in Christ, which was a divine secret until Christ revealed it (see Ephesians 1:7-10). A measure of the hiddenness of the Old Testament's spiritual meaning is the surprise of Jesus' contemporaries, including his disciples, to his revelation of it.

Although the spiritual meaning is hidden, it is not subjective or imaginary. It is a meaning that God has placed there. As with the literal meaning, so with the spiritual meaning: we cannot attribute to the Bible whatever meaning we like. When scriptural writers or the official teachers of the Church have found meanings in Scripture that would not have been apparent to the original writers, they were not giving to these passages whatever meanings they chose. The Spirit was guiding them to perceive meanings which had earlier been hidden. The spiritual sense is discerned by divine revelation, given first by

Christ to his disciples and then by the Spirit to the Church.

In an attempt to unearth the spiritual meanings of the Old Testament, Christians ever since Clement of Alexandria in the second century have offered allegorical interpretations. Teachers have used allegorical interpretation to show how everything from the number of Jacob's sons in Genesis to the appearance of the beloved's teeth in the Song of Songs speak about Christ and Christian life. To what extent can we take this approach as a guide for discovering the spiritual meaning of the Bible?

St. Augustine and St. Thomas Aquinas allowed for great freedom of interpretation: so long as the reader stayed within the bounds of the teaching of the Church and the rule of charity, any interpretation might be entertained. Nevertheless, some of these allegorical interpretations of writers of the past seem today to be projections into the text rather than discoveries drawing out of the text meanings that it contains. Indeed, some of the allegorizing has been somewhat fanciful. It may well be, after all, that not every verse of the Old Testament has a spiritual meaning, and the insistence on finding one leads inevitably to questionable results. Celestin Charlier says that the Fathers emphasized the fundamental themes of Christian faith, "but in the margin they devised a whole mass of flourishes, variations, and improvisations which could be called semi-poetic flights of fancy" (*The Christian Approach to the Bible*, page 268).

The imaginative quality of allegorizing interpretations does not make them useless. For one thing, the Fathers and later writers who used the Old Testament in an allegorical way did not necessarily assert that they were drawing out meanings objectively present in the text. Often they were simply employing biblical imagery and events as the language in which to discuss God, prayer, spiritual life, and so on. An imaginative, even playful, allegorical use of Scripture is sometimes helpful in order to give details in the Bible an application to our lives. It may be useful for private meditation and reflection, occasionally even for preaching, provided that it is not overindulged. Pius XII warned preachers against substituting this sort of allegorizing for interpretation which brings out the meaning of the inspired authors (*Divino Afflante Spiritu*).

If, however, we seek the real spiritual meaning of Scripture, we must rely not on our imaginations or those of figures of the past. As John Paul II has written, since not just any spiritual sense can be attributed to the text, it requires scholarly, theological investigation to determine the spiritual sense (in Pontifical Biblical Commission, *The Interpretation of the Bible in the Church*). The fundamental guides to the spiritual sense of the Old Testament are the words and deeds of Jesus and the interpretations of the New Testament writers. Beyond this, there are the points of agreement among the Fathers and the teaching of the popes and the councils of the Church. The liturgy and the sacramental rites, which take up texts of the Old Testament and apply them to Christ and life in him, are likewise trustworthy indicators of the spiritual sense of Scripture.

Celestin Charlier suggests that the spiritual meaning of the Old Testament is better seen in larger themes and developments than in single words or elements. For example, what makes Joshua a prefigurement, or "type," of Jesus is not his name (which in the Hebrew is the same as "Jesus") but his role as the one who secures the land for God's people. David is a type of Christ not because of the stones in his sling (as symbols of Jesus, "the stone that made men stumble") but because he served as king of God's people with a heart set on the Lord.

Chapter Eight

How Can It Speak to Me?
The Bible in Your Life

In the Byzantine liturgy, before the people go forward to receive Communion, the priest holds out the chalice and intones: "Approach with fear of God and with faith." These words might suitably sound in our ears as we open the Bible. In the Bible, as in Holy Communion, Jesus, the living Word of God, comes to us and draws us to himself. Reading the Bible, like receiving Communion, is a response to his personal love for us. It makes sense to approach with "fear of God" and "faith."

Fear of God means reverence and awe, not cringing timidity or anxiety about punishment. Reverence is appropriate when we read the Bible because in its words we encounter God, who is mystery beyond comprehension. In the words of the human authors and editors, the God who created us speaks to us. That *is* awesome!

Fear of God also means obedience and trust in him (see Genesis 22:12). God being the creator, and we being the creatures, distrust and unwillingness to obey are out of place in our relationship with him. The biblical writers acknowledge how difficult we humans find it to trustfully surrender ourselves to God. But they encourage us with the counsel that "the fear

"The Church has always venerated the divine Scriptures as she venerated the Body of the Lord." *Dogmatic Constitution on Divine Revelation*, section 21.

of the Lord is the beginning of wisdom" (Proverbs 9:10; see Job 28:28; Psalm 111:10; Sirach 1:16). Deciding to put our lives in God's hands and cooperate with him is the starting point for hearing his words to us, and thus the starting point for reading the Bible. Indeed, in the Bible true hearing *is* obeying; the two are inseparable—as indicated by the biblical writers' use of "hear" to mean "hear and obey" (see Deuteronomy 4:1). If we wish to truly hear God as we read the Bible, we must open it with a willingness to respond to what we will find there.

As to *faith*, the key to reading the Bible as God's word to you is simply to believe that it *is* God's word to you. The belief is well-founded. God continues to unfold the plan of salvation recounted in the Bible—and he calls each of us to be part of it. He has a role for you to play. The words that he spoke to participants in earlier stages of his plan are now his words to you, who participate in a later stage of the same divine plan.

Our faith that God will speak to us as we read the Bible is grounded in the presence of the Holy Spirit. The Spirit moved the men and women of the old covenant to hear and respond to God's words. Through the Spirit, the Son took flesh and carried out his ministry. The Son gave the Spirit to the community of his followers. This Spirit now makes us the living body of Christ. In the worship of the Church, the Spirit transforms the bread and wine of the Eucharistic offering into the living Christ. This same Spirit brings the words of Scripture to life for us.

Scripture is an inspired and inspiring word. Just as God inspired the Bible's authors and editors, so he wishes to inspire the readers. This does not mean that we will have a distinct sense of God's guidance or an unusual experience of his love every time we read the Bible. It is doubtful that the authors and editors had any special experience as they composed the biblical writings. Our reading of the Bible is an ordinary human experience, as the writing seems to have been an ordinary human experience. But just as God worked through the authors' praying, thinking, writing, and rewriting, so he will work through our reading, studying, pondering, and praying. In its own way, Bible reading, like the Bible itself, is a divine-human reality. As we read the Bible, God works through the human abilities he has given us to accomplish things that go far beyond human abilities. The Spirit will lead us to know God and love him, to believe and hope in him.

If we come to Scripture with "fear of God and faith," God will reveal himself to us. The process requires desire on our part, patience in letting God reveal himself as he will, and readiness to respond when he does so. "Blessed are the pure in heart, for they will see God" (Matthew 5:8).

Just Read It!

After all the preceding chapters of explanation about the history and interpretation of the Bible, we arrive at a very practical point. *We need to read it!* And, since we have a daily need to hear God's word, we need to read the Bible daily. The Bible is deep and broad, and sometimes difficult, and only through regular reading will we be able to gradually grow in understanding it. Quite simply, the most important decision you can make regarding the Bible is to make it a regular part of your daily routine.

Are you willing to give the Bible priority amid the other pressing matters in your life? The psalmist appeals to us, "O that today you would listen to his voice! Do not harden your hearts"

(Psalm 95:7-8). The first question this exhortation raises is not, "Will you harden your heart against God's voice?" but "Will you listen to his voice today?" God is speaking. Will you take the time to listen?

This question needs a specific answer, an answer that specifies a particular time and a particular place. Exactly *when* and *where* will you read the Bible today and tomorrow and the next day? For most of us, the only way to answer these questions is to identify a regular time and place for reading the Bible that will work for us every day. What is this time and place for you?

I suggest aiming for fifteen to twenty minutes a day. Less than this is probably too little to collect your thoughts and make any progress. More than this may go beyond what most of us can squeeze into our busy lives. Better to set a realistic goal and stick with it than fail in the attempt to reach a higher goal. With reading the Bible, as with learning a language, better a little *every* day than a longer period less frequently. Somewhere, somehow, just about every one of us can find fifteen to twenty minutes each day to read the Bible. And with determination and God's help, we can stay with it.

The goal in our daily reading is not to read as much as possible but to understand and apply what we read. Thus we need to read carefully and thoughtfully. This means adopting a slower pace than we use in reading a newspaper or a novel. Reading the Bible is more like walking down a street than driving on an expressway. Read a section through, then read it again more slowly, asking questions about meaning. Pause, linger. Bible reading, George Martin has written, is "leisurely reading, reading with attention to detail" (*Reading Scripture As the Word of God*, page 16).

Growing in Understanding

The Bible is written for everyone, but nothing in it says that anyone can simply pick it up and read with total understanding. As the preceding chapters have shown, every one of us needs help to understand the Bible. Help is not something that only the exceptionally ignorant need; it is not something we may expect to outgrow. Reading the Bible with help is normal. Obviously, as Raymond Brown once remarked, "God can speak to the reader without the permission of scholars" (*Responses to 101 Questions on the Bible*, page 23). But to gain an in-depth understanding, we need the support of scholars, saints, and other teachers of the past and present. Reading the Bible is like going on a guided tour. You go in order to see for yourself, but you go with a guide who can help you understand what you see.

We read the Bible as members of the community of the Bible, the Church. This is true even when we read the Bible in solitude. When we are by ourselves, other members of the community can be present with us through their written words—in the introductions and notes in the version of the Bible that we use, in commentaries, in devotional guides and other sorts of help. These resources enable us to read the Bible within the faith of the Church.

All this means that reading the Bible involves a study component. Study, of course, requires effort—an effort that we may chafe at. We tend to want Scripture to be simple because we want our relationship with God to be simple. At root, both are simple. But then, in their full expression, both are also complex. The events through which God has acted in history are complex. The world God has created and we ourselves are endlessly complex. It would be unreasonable to expect that the

Bible would not also be complex. To grow in understanding and maturity in life is a long, difficult process. A long process also stretches before us as we seek to understand and respond to God's word in Scripture.

To think that the Spirit will override the complexity and give us infused knowledge as we sit by ourselves with a Bible without any notes or other help is a kind of super spiritualism—expecting God to circumvent the natural processes that he has created. He has given us minds because he wants us to use them. The authors and editors had to observe, ponder, listen, pray, write, edit. We, too, have to invest some effort if we are to learn from their words. God did not simply dictate the Bible to human stenographers; he does not simply unveil all the mysteries communicated in Scripture to us without our having to use ordinary human means to understand.

While the Bible requires study, it does not require us to become scholars. True, it has depths that will keep us learning and growing for a lifetime; but it was not written for academics or geniuses. The Bible was written for ordinary people, and with modest help all of us can read it with understanding. Steve Mueller has observed that "The most common fear when approaching the formidable journey of Bible reading is that we are not smart enough"(*The Seeker's Guide to Reading the Bible*, page 21). But we are. Mueller adds, "You don't have to become an expert on the Bible, but you do need to become a more competent reader." That is a realistic goal for all of us. Keep at it; don't get discouraged. The Bible makes more sense the more acquainted with it you become.

As we begin to read the Bible, we discover that there is a lot we do not understand—and we will continue to have this experience no matter how much we learn. After years of reading, my knowledge of the Bible seems like small islands in an ocean of ignorance. This can be unnerving or discouraging, but it need not be. We should focus on what we do understand, and not be disturbed by all that we do not. If we take a gradual, persevering approach, our islands of knowledge will slowly grow.

What we do understand always gives us more than enough instruction to act on. Some of the Bible is hard to grasp; other parts are actually easy to understand but hard to do. It is not difficult to see what Jesus is driving at when he says to love not only those who do us good but also those who do us harm (see Luke 6:27-36), but it is exceedingly difficult to put this into practice. No matter how slowly our comprehension of Scripture grows, we will never run out of sections that we already understand but have not yet fully applied to our lives. No one has ever gotten to the point where he or she could say, "I've carried out all the parts of Scripture that I understand. I would be willing to apply more of it to my life, if only I could understand it!"

Responding to what we understand in the Bible is a crucial part of growing in understanding. Some of what we do not grasp at our present point in life is obscure to us because of our present immaturity, our worldliness, our selfishness. These flaws prevent us from comprehending more deeply the Bible's message of God's love. The scholars on the Pontifical Biblical Commission observe that "As the reader matures in the life of the Spirit, there grows also his or her capacity to understand the realities of which the Bible speaks" (*The Interpretation of the Bible in the Church*). Indeed, as we grow in love for God, Scripture itself seems to grow.

What Does It Mean for Me?

Of course, study is not the be-all and end-all of our time with the Bible. It is a means to an end. We study so that we may understand. We understand so that we may live the lives God wants us to live and arrive at the goal God wants us to attain. Once we have some idea of what Scripture means, we go on to ponder what it means for us.

The basic question is, "How does what I am reading in the Bible relate to my life here and now?" Occasionally the answer will leap from the text and address us so clearly and directly that it will seem that God has written the passage just for us. More often, we need to do some thinking in order to discover the connections between the biblical text and ourselves. God speaks to us through the Bible not only in the moments of sudden, powerful insight, but also gradually, almost imperceptibly, in the process of reflection.

Various questions can help us find points of contact between the biblical text and our twenty-first-century lives. When have I experienced anything like what the people in the text experienced? How does my experience help me understand

"As seekers, we cannot just skim the surface, amassing bits of unconnected information. Despite promises we often hear, there is no instant wisdom. Genuine wisdom requires the patient process of seeing the connections between facts and relating them to form the bigger picture. Bible literacy is measured by assimilation, not accumulation." Steve Mueller, *The Seeker's Guide to Reading the Bible*, page 187.

their thoughts and feelings? What aspects of my life today do these words of the Bible lead me to consider? (The text speaks of forgiveness. Who have I failed to forgive?) How does this passage of Scripture cause me to evaluate these aspects of my life? What can I learn from the way people in this passage responded, or failed to respond, to God?

We can try putting ourselves into the text. One way to do this is to recreate the scene in our imagination, place ourselves within it, and then observe what happens. How does it affect me? How inclined am I to act in the situation? What do I wish to say to the Lord? Another approach is to identify with a participant in the narrative. For example, take the parable of the father with two sons (see Luke 15:11-32). The son who rejects his father—that is me! How, then, do the father's words to him speak to me? The son who stays with the father but is angry at him—that's me too! How do the father's words to *him* speak to me? The father who is patient with both his wayward sons—that also is me! Whose weaknesses am I called to be patient with?

Some people find it useful to explore questions like these over a period of time by keeping a journal. Some find that discussion of the Bible with other people is helpful for digging out its implications for life today: when I hear how other people are detecting God's word to them in the Bible, I am led to see how he is speaking to me also.

"One of the great thrills of reading the Bible ... is the recognition that the biblical situation is similar to our own. What God demanded by way of response in times past, He is still demanding today." Raymond E. Brown, S.S., *Responses to 101 Questions on the Bible*, page 28.

Pray

Bible reading is an opportunity for encounter with God. "In the sacred books the Father who is in heaven comes lovingly to meet his children, and talks with them," the bishops at Vatican Council II wrote. Thus, prayer should accompany our reading of the Bible, "so that God and man may talk together" (*Dogmatic Constitution on Divine Revelation*, sections 21, 25). We need the help of the Church, the assistance of scholars, the guidance of one another to understand the Bible and to see how it applies to our lives. But each of us has the responsibility to seek God as we read his word. No one can meet him for us.

In fact, the Bible is a perfect starting point for prayer. Prayer begins with listening to God and perceiving what he has done for us, and, as we have seen, this is exactly where the Bible puts the accent. It speaks first about what God has done for us, and frames everything that we must do as a response to his initiative. To ponder Scripture is to consider what God has done. This is the basis for all prayer. Every passage of Scripture issues a call to conversion. Conversion, turning back to God, is based on our recognition that the saving events of Scripture are continued in our lives today. God gives us life today, calls us and makes promises to us, rescues us, comes to us. It is because God has already drawn us into his saving plan, that we can make any response to him.

"Te totum applica ad textum. Rem totam applica ad te. Apply your whole self to the text. Apply the whole text to yourself." J.A. Bengel

Prayer weaves naturally in and out of our Bible reading, study, reflection. There is no formula for praying Scripture, for there is no formula for praying. Prayer is conversation with God, but the essence of the conversation lies not in words but in an interaction between persons deeper than any words—an attentiveness, trust, love. In the phrase of Cardinal John Henry Newman, "Heart speaks to heart."

Scripture leads us to this encounter with God in a multitude of ways. It can awe us with the scope and profundity of his love for the human race, displayed in the entire sweep of revelation. It can shatter our independence and pride with a single word that seems to have been written precisely for us. It provides us with prayers to pray—the psalms and numerous other prayers and hymns scattered throughout the Old and New Testament. We are invited to meditate on the truths God reveals, to chew on particular words and phrases, to recreate in our imagination the scenes that are described, to sit in silent wonder, to thank, to praise.

The most profound praying of Scripture takes place in the celebration of the Eucharist. Scripture recounts and interprets God's saving deeds in history. In the Eucharistic liturgy, God's deeds are remembered in an act of public thanksgiving. The climax of God's saving deeds—Jesus' death and resurrection—becomes present anew. In the Eucharist, we enter into Jesus' offering of himself to the Father, which reconciles the human

"Whoever thinks that he understands the divine Scriptures or any part of them so that it does not build the double love of God and of our neighbor does not understand it at all." St. Augustine, *On Christian Doctrine*, 1:36.

race to God and restores our union with God lost through sin. We join in the heavenly liturgy of praise which saints and angels offer to God for all eternity. We eat the bread of eternal life, Jesus' life-giving body and blood, and experience a foretaste of the banquet that he will will share with us in the kingdom of God. Thus in the Eucharist we enter into the central event of Scripture and experience the divine life into which Scripture guides us. The Eucharist brings us into communion with the Lord of Scripture and provides us with the most profound opportunity to express our gratitude for his love.

Chapter Nine

Where Do I Start?

Buying a Bible and
Finding Your Way Around in It

To read the Bible, you must have a Bible. There are many different translations and editions of the Bible available. How can you choose among them? Our discussion so far suggests these criteria.

- **A Bible with all its parts.** Since the Catholic canon of the Old Testament contains more books than the canon recognized by Protestants (see pages 74–76), select a version that contains all the Old Testament books recognized by the Catholic Church. Every version prepared under Catholic aupices has the entire Catholic Old Testament; some versions prepared under Protestant and ecumenical auspices do too—but not all. Check the table of contents against the Old Testament listing of books on page 14.

- **A version in harmony with the Church.** In order to read the Bible with the Church, select a version that has an "imprimatur" on the copyright page. This indicates that a Catholic bishop has determined that nothing in the translation, introductions, or notes conflicts with the Church's teaching and tradition. Every version prepared under Catholic auspices will have an imprimatur; so will some editions prepared under Protestant and ecumenical auspices.

- **A study Bible.** Hopefully the preceding chapters have persuaded you that we all need help to read the Bible with understanding. The most convenient form for that help is a study Bible. A study Bible contains extensive introductory articles, notes at the bottom or in the margins of the page, maps, and other resources. A study Bible is different from a "reader's edition," which supplies few or no notes, and from a "devotional" Bible, which incorporates extra material to help you reflect on how the Bible might apply to your life but does not shed much light on what the Bible means. The bishops at Vatican II said that scholars and publishers ought to produce versions of the Bible "furnished with necessary and truly adequate explanations" so that we can become "familiar with the sacred Scriptures and steeped in their spirit" (*Dogmatic Constitution on Divine Revelation*, section 25). That's a study Bible.

- **A modern translation.** The Bible is sometimes difficult to understand; we don't need translations that add to the difficulties. We need translations that employ all available scholarly resources to put the Hebrew, Aramaic, and Greek texts into clear, comprehensible English. Older translations have their value, but are not suitable as the main translation that we use for study (see box, pages 126–127).

Put these four criteria together, and where does that leave you? To be honest, without a lot of options. At the time that I am writing, only two English editions of the Bible meet all these criteria. While there are several modern translations that contain the entire Catholic Old Testament and are approved for Catholic use, only two of them are adult study Bibles. They are the *Catholic Study Bible* and the *Catholic Bible: Personal Study Edition*, both published by Oxford University Press. Both carry a wealth of introductory material (hundreds of pages), helpful notes, and other material. Both use the New American Bible translation, which was produced and revised in the last forty years. Not quite a study Bible but containing a good deal of help—the introductory articles are slight but there are ample notes—is the New Jerusalem Bible (get the *full* edition, not the "standard" or "reader's" editions, which strip out the intros and notes). There is also a Catholic study Bible designed for young people, the *Catholic Youth Bible*, which uses the New Revised Standard Version.

My first, very strong, recommendation is to get a study Bible. My second recommendation is to get another Bible, using a different translation. No translation is perfect. Each has strengths and weaknesses. You will get a better understanding of many biblical passages by reading them in more than one translation. Doing so is like seeing with two eyes instead of one. As St. Augustine observed, "An inspection of various translations frequently makes obscure passages clear." On the other hand, sometimes the two translations will be so different that they will leave you puzzled about the meaning of a passage. But this, too, may be valuable, for it is probably a signal that the underlying biblical text is ambiguous or obscure—and, therefore, you should be cautious in interpreting and applying it.

Since your second translation is to be supplementary, it need not be a study Bible. What factors might you take into account in choosing a second Bible? Here are a couple of considerations:

- **Word-for-word or thought-for-thought?** Translators go in one of two directions. Either they try to enable the reader to see the word choices and grammatical structures of the original as much as possible, or they try to recreate the effect of the original in modern English. The first approach, which seeks "formal equivalence," tends to translate the original text word-for-word and phrase-for-phrase. The second approach, called "dynamic equivalence," translates thought-for-thought and sentence-for-sentence (see box). Between the two approaches, there is no right or wrong. Each has advantages and disadvantages. Where the underlying text is ambiguous or obscure, the formal-equivalence translation will tend to reflect the ambiguity or obscurity so that you can see what it is. Seeking to produce a translation that is easy to understand, a dynamic-equivalence translation will tend to settle on one possible interpretation. Thus a word-for-word translation is better for study but, if you already have a study Bible, you might want your second translation to be of the thought-for-thought variety, which is easier for meditation and prayer.

Formal and Dynamic Equivalence Compared

Here are four translations of Romans 12:1-2. The first two are examples of a formal equivalence, or word-for-word, approach. The last two are examples of dynamic equivalence, or thought-for-thought translation.

"And now, brothers, I beg you through the mercy of God to offer your bodies as a living sacrifice holy and acceptable to God, your spiritual worship. Do not conform yourselves to this age but be transformed by the renewal of your mind, so that you may judge what is God's will, what is good, pleasing and perfect." *New American Bible*

"I appeal to you therefore, brothers and sisters, by the mercies of God, to present your bodies as a living sacrifice, holy and acceptable to God, which is your spiritual worship. Do not be conformed to this world, but be transformed by the renewing of your minds, so that you may discern what is the will of God—what is good and acceptable and perfect." *New Revised Standard Version*

"I urge you, then, brothers, remembering the mercies of God, to offer your bodies as a living sacrifice, dedicated and acceptable to God; that is the kind of worship for you, as sensible people. Do not model your behaviour on the contemporary world, but let the renewing of your minds transform you, so that you may discern for yourselves what is the will of God—what is good and acceptable and mature." *New Jerusalem Bible*

"Therefore, my brothers, I implore you by God's mercy to offer your very selves to him: a living sacrifice, dedicated and fit for his acceptance, the worship offered by mind and heart. Adapt yourselves no longer to the pattern of this present world, but let your minds be remade and your whole nature thus transformed. Then you will be able to discern the will of God, and to know what is good, acceptable, and perfect." *New English Bible*

- **Gender language.** Traditionally, English sometime uses masculine pronouns to refer to both men and women. In recent decades, many people have rejected this approach, in the belief that it excludes women, while other people have vigorously defended it. There are complex linguistic and cultural arguments on both sides of the issue. Here, too, the reader's taste plays the major role in making a choice. But there are some things to be aware of. Those who prefer the older approach, in which masculine pronouns are used generically for men and women, now have a limited range of translations to choose from, and these translations are not based on the most up-to-date scholarship. One must choose the older Revised Standard Version, for example, rather than the more recent New Revised Standard Version. Those who prefer the new approach, in which masculine pronouns are not used generically for people or even for God, should be aware that such translations sometimes blur the meaning of the underlying Hebrew, Aramaic, and Greek texts, all of which use masculine pronouns this way. Translators may render a third-person singular (he/him) as second-person (you) or third-person plural (they). "Inclusive language" translations may obscure connections between passages in the Old and New Testaments, as, for example, when the New Revised Standard Version translates "son of man" as "human beings" in Hebrews 2:6, making it impossible to see that the author is connecting Psalm 8 with Jesus. At times "inclusive language" translations misrepresent the culture, as when the New Revised Standard Version renders "son" or "lad" as "children" in passages referring to physical discipline. As John J. Pilch points out, girls were never subjected to the kind of physical discipline imposed on boys (*Choosing a Bible Translation*, page 20).

It is easy to acquire several translations at once by buying a parallel Bible, which presents four or more translations side by side. A good selection is *The Complete Parallel Bible* from

Oxford University Press, which contains the New Revised Standard Version, the Revised English Bible, the New American Bible, and the New Jerusalem Bible.

A final word of advice. Avoid paraphrases, such as the *Living Bible*, abridgements, such as the *Reader's Digest Bible*, and translations that distort the meaning in order to promote a religious or cultural cause, such as the translation of the Jehovah's Witnesses (New World Translation) and *The New Testament and Psalms: An Inclusive Version*. The latter version tries to avoid calling God "Father" or Jesus "Son," with the result that Jesus speaks of himself as "the Child" (John 3:35) and prays in Gethsemane: "Father-Mother, if you are willing, remove this cup from me" (Luke 22:42). This translation also suppresses the sex of some of the people whom Jesus meets, so that Jesus heals a "person" who is paralyzed (Mark 2:1-12) and a "person" who is deaf (Mark 7:31-37). In this translation, the Church is no longer the bride of Christ (see Ephesians 5:25-32; Revelation 21:2).

Recent English Translations of the Bible

Word-for-word translations	**Thought-for-thought translations**
Revised Standard Version	Jerusalem Bible
New Revised Standard Version	New Jerusalem Bible
	New English Bible
New American Bible	Revised English Bible
New International Version	Today's English Version
New American Standard Bible	(Good News Bible)
	Contemporary English Version
New Jewish Version	

Older is Not Better

Two seventeenth-century English translations of Scripture continue to have special prominence. The King James Version is a masterpiece of English poetry and prose, worth reading for its literary quality and influence on English literary tradition. The King James Version was translated by Protestant scholars at a time when Protestants and Catholics were at loggerheads, and sometimes at swords points, over theological issues. It was not acceptable to Catholics, and so Catholics produced their own translation, called the Douay-Rheims Version. Some Catholics continue to rely on it, partly because it has a greater solemnity and gravity than modern translations. However, both translations are out of date.

- In the last four centuries, scholars have learned a great deal about ancient languages and cultures and have identified more accurate copies of the Hebrew, Aramaic, and Greek texts of the Bible. All this enables them to produce more accurate translations—translations that bring us closer to the inspired authors' meaning.

- English has changed a lot since these translations were made. Numerous words have shifted meaning. Seventeenth-century English is no longer the best vehicle for conveying meaning to twenty-first century readers. As Fr. Peter M.J. Stravinskas writes, "While there may be a certain mystique about archaic language, it does much to obscure the meaning of the text" (*The Catholic Church and the Bible*, page 29).

- Even where the old translations are reasonably accurate and comprehensible, they make the Bible sound like an old book. But the New Testament writings, and much of the Old Testament, sounded lively and contemporary to their first readers.
- A further problem with the Douay version is that it is a translation of a translation (an English translation of a Latin version) rather than a translation direct from the original Hebrew, Aramaic, and Greek texts. As long ago as 1943, Pope Pius XII established the norm that Catholic translations should be made from the original languages in order to reflect as accurately as possible the meaning of the inspired authors and editors. The bishops at Vatican II emphasized the importance of "correct translations" produced "principally from the original texts of the sacred books" (*Dogmatic Constitution on Divine Revelation*, section 22).

Find Your Way Around

Once you have a Bible, you need to learn how to navigate within it.

A numbered system of longer and shorter divisions facilitates finding material. The books are divided into sections called chapters, which may be a page or two in length. Chapters are subdivided into "verses," containing a sentence or two (not only the poetry but also the prose is divided into "verses"). The division into chapters and verses, and therefore the numbering system, was worked out only in the Middle Ages and is not part of the inspired text. The system is imperfect: for various reasons, there are small discrepancies between editions regarding the divisions and numbering of the chapters and verses. So sometimes you may have to look backward or forward a verse or two to find the verse you are looking for (in the Psalms the numbering systems may diverge by an entire psalm).

In citing biblical texts it is common to abbreviate the names of the biblical books and to use a shorthand method of referring to the chapter and verse. Unfortunately, there is more than one system of abbreviation and more than one approach to representing the chapter and verse numbers. For example, the first verse of the twelfth chapter of Genesis might be represented as Gen 12:1, Gen 12.1, or Gen xii 1. Genesis might also be abbreviated Gn.

A complication is that not only the abbreviation systems but the names of some biblical books vary. For example, the book sometimes called the Song of Songs is also called the Song of Solomon and the Canticle of Canticles. Ecclesiastes is sometimes called Qoheleth; Ecclesiasticus is sometimes called Sirach. As you would expect, the abbreviations vary accordingly.

These problems are relatively minor, however. It should take just a few minutes to determine how the version that you are using handles titles, abbreviations, and numbers for chapters and verses. As a starting point, check the table of contents or list of books and abbreviations at the front of your Bible. While you are looking at the table of contents, you might also compare the order of the Old Testament books to the list on page 14. Unlike the list on that page, some versions place the material accepted by Catholics but not by Protestants together between the Old and New Testaments or after the end of the New Testament (such versions also sometimes include a few books that neither

Catholics nor Protestants regard as Scripture, such as 1 and 2 Esdras).

It pays to get acquainted with the introductions, notes, maps, and other helps.

Introductory articles usually contain material about the date, the authorship, the literary form, and the setting of the book. At first glance, this may look dry and boring. But hopefully you now see how such information, which sheds light on the type, background, situation and purpose, and structure of the writing, is useful for understanding what the authors and editors meant.

Depending on the layout of your version, it may have as many as three sets of notes accompanying the biblical text, either at the foot of the page or in the margin. One set may give information about the text or translation. For instance, after Psalm 85:8, which the Revised Standard Version renders "...to those who turn to him in their hearts," the RSV has this note: "Gk: Heb *but let them not turn back to folly.*" The note tells us that the translators have followed a Greek version but supplies us with the meaning of the Hebrew text.

A second set of notes may contain cross references. These will lead you to passages in Scripture that are somehow related. Many cross-references accompanying the Old Testament will point to passages in the New Testament concerning Jesus and the life of the Church. Accompanying Psalm 2, for example, you will find cross-references to the several uses of this prayer in the New Testament. Thus cross-references are useful for reading the parts of the Bible in light of the whole and, especially, for perceiving the spiritual meaning, as we discussed in chapter seven.

A third set of notes—often the longest of the three—may offer background information, explanations, and other comments.

Develop a Reading Plan

Although the whole Bible is God's word, not every part of it is equally important. The Gospels are of central importance. The other parts are subordinate to them. Thus we are not obliged to devote as much attention to every part. Indeed, we should not. We should focus our attention on what is most important.

In addition, not every part of the Bible is equally interesting or accessible to us. This should not be a source of guilt. If you find portions of the Bible hard going, skip them with a clear conscience. Come back at a later date, after you have explored biblical books that are more congenial to you.

Where to begin? My advice is to begin wherever you like. Some experts criticize the begin-at-the-beginning approach, because many first-time Bible readers who start with Genesis, get bogged down somewhere in Exodus or Leviticus, and give up. But then, there are readers who feel uncomfortable beginning a book anywhere except the beginning and who are not deterred by stretches of dry material. Some people advise beginners to start with the Gospel of Luke or with Luke's companion volume, Acts of the Apostles. Certainly either of those makes an excellent starting point, but there are many others.

I suggest, however, that once you select a biblical book, you read it in its entirety. (Exceptions would be very long books, such as Psalms and Isaiah.) Only by reading a biblical book all the way through can you get its overall message and see how the parts fit into the whole. I also suggest alternating between the

New Testament and the Old Testament. If you alternate between the testaments, you will complete your reading of the New Testament first, because there are fewer New Testament books. Then you can go on to reread the New Testament books while you continue reading Old Testament books for the first time. This sort of emphasis on the New Testament is appropriate for a follower of Christ.

If you stick with it, you will gradually get used to the atmosphere, the background, the themes of the biblical books. As when you move to another part of the country or live abroad, the strange becomes familiar little by little. If you stay long enough, you begin to feel at home.

Continue Your Education

Keep a learner's attitude. Be on the lookout for talks, courses, TV programs, videos, books, magazine articles, and so on that offer background and insights into the Bible. Accumulate some tools for study, or at least get to know where they are at a parish or public library. The following are basic tools (for specific recommendations, see the next chapter):

- **Bible Dictionary.** This will give you short articles on words, people, places, events, biblical books, and so on. A good single-volume Bible dictionary is an invaluable companion to reading the Bible.
- **Commentaries**. A single-volume commentary will provide a brief chapter-by-chapter explanation of all the books of the Bible. There are also commentary series, in which an entire commentary may be devoted to a single biblical book.

- **Material for reflection and application**. Devotional Bibles, books, periodicals, and pamphlets can aid your discussion and journaling, reflection and prayer. Somewhere out there are materials that will suit your taste.
- **The *Catechism of the Catholic Church*.** The *Catechism* will help you explore how the issues that you encounter in your reading of the Bible have developed in the Catholic tradition. (See the topical and biblical indexes in the back of the *Catechism*.)
- **Atlas.** I never travel without a road map. Why read the Bible without some maps at hand?
- **Concordance.** A concordance shows all the passages in the Bible where each word is used. This makes it handy for locating passages. It is also useful for finding passages that discuss a given person or event or idea, and thus for investigating how various biblical authors may have talked about them

Chapter Ten

Where Do I Go From Here?
Resources for Study, Reflection, and Prayer

A. Introductions to the Bible

Lawrence Boadt, *Reading the Old Testament* (New York: Paulist Press, 1985).

Dom Celestin Charlier, *The Christian Approach to the Bible,* John M.T. Barton, trans. (New York: Paulist Press, 1967).

Michael Duggan, *The Consuming Fire: A Christian Introduction to the Old Testament* (San Francisco: Ignatius Press, 1991).

Jerome Kodell, O.S.B., *The Catholic Bible Study Handbook* (Ann Arbor, Mich.: Servant Publications, 1985).

George Martin, *Reading Scripture As the Word of God: Practical Approaches and Attitudes* (Ann Arbor, Mich.: Servant Publications, 1998).

Steve Mueller, *The Seeker's Guide to Reading the Bible: A Catholic View* (Chicago: Loyola Press, 1999).

Pheme Perkins, *Reading the New Testament* (New York: Paulist Press, 1988).

John Rogerson, *An Introduction to the Bible* (New York: Penguin Putnam Inc., 1999).

B. Catholic Church documents

Austin P. Flannery, O.P., ed., *Vatican Council II: The Conciliar and Post Conciliar Documents* (Grand Rapids, Mich.: William B. Eerdmans Publishing Co., 1984). This book contains the *Dogmatic Constitution on Divine Revelation*.

Joseph A. Fitzmyer, S.J., *The Biblical Commission's Document, "The Interpretation of the Bible in the Church": Text and Commentary* (Rome: Editrice Pontificio Instituto Biblico, 1995). This book contains the Pontifical Biblical Commission's 1993 statement, *The Interpretation of the Bible in the Church,* along with statements by Pope John Paul II and Cardinal Joseph Ratzinger on biblical interpretation, and a commentary by Joseph Fitzmyer. The text of *The Interpretation of the Bible in the Church,* by the Pontifical Biblical Commission, with the comments by the pope and Cardinal Ratzinger, but without the commentary by Father Fitzmyer, is available from the United States Catholic Conference, in Washington, D.C.

Catechism of the Catholic Church (Washington, D.C.: United States Catholic Conference—Libreria Editrice Vaticana, 2000).

C. Tools for biblical study
1. Adult Catholic study Bibles

Jean Marie Hiesberger and others, eds., *The Catholic Bible: Personal Study Edition* (New York: Oxford University Press, 1997).

Donald Senior and others, eds., *The Catholic Study Bible* (New York: Oxford University Press, 1990).

2. Dictionaries and other one-volume companions to the Bible
Paul J. Achtemeier and others, eds., *The HarperCollins Bible Dictionary* (San Francisco: HarperCollins, 1996).

Bruce M. Metzger and Michael D. Coogan, eds., *The Oxford Companion to the Bible* (New York: Oxford University Press, 1993).

Carroll Stuhlmueller, C.P., ed., *The Collegeville Pastoral Dictionary of Biblical Theology* (Collegeville, Minn.: The Liturgical Press, 1996).

Geoffrey Wigoder and others, eds., *Illustrated Dictionary and Concordance of the Bible* (New York: Macmillan Publishing Company, 1986).

Geoffrey Wigoder, Shalom M. Paul, and Benedict T. Viviano, O.P., *Almanac of the Bible* (New York: Prentice Hall, 1991).

3. Atlases
Yohanan Aharoni and Michael Avi-Yonah, *The Macmillan Bible Atlas* (New York: Macmillan Publishing Co., 1993).

James B. Pritchard, *The HarperCollins Concise Atlas of the Bible* (San Francisco: HarperCollins, 1991).

John Rogerson, *Atlas of the Bible* (New York: Facts on File Publications, 1985).

4. Concordances

Each concordance is keyed to a particular translation. The following concordances are keyed to the New Revised Standard Version:

NRSV Exhaustive Concordance (Nashville, Tenn.: Thomas Nelson Publishers, 1991).

The NRSV Concordance Unabridged (Grand Rapids, Mich.: Zondervan Publishing House, 1991).

5. One-volume commentaries of the entire Catholic Bible

Dianne Bergant and Robert J. Karris, O.F.M., eds., *The Collegeville Bible Commentary* (Collegeville, Minn.: The Liturgical Press, 1989).

Raymond E. Brown, S.S., Joseph A. Fitzmyer, S.J., and Roland E. Murphy, O.Carm., eds., *The New Jerome Biblical Commentary* (Englewood Cliffs, N.J.: Prentice Hall, 1990).

James L. Mays and others, eds., *Harper's Bible Commentary* (San Francisco: HarperCollins, 1988).

6. Other commentaries

Sacra Pagina series. The Liturgical Press (see section D for address).

Spiritual Commentaries series. New City Press (see section D for address).

Commentaries by Church Fathers

The following series of books contain volumes by Church Fathers on Scripture along with other patristic works:

The Fathers of the Church series. Among this series' patristic biblical commentaries is the commentary of St. John Chrysostom on Genesis. Catholic University Press (see section D for address).

Ancient Christian Writers series. Among this series' patristic biblical commentaries are the commentaries of St. Augustine on Psalms and on the Sermon on the Mount. Paulist Press (see section D for address).

Some of the biblical homilies of St. John Chrysostom have been published by St. Vladimir's Seminary Press (see section D for address).

7. Materials for discussion, reflection, and meditation
"6 Weeks with the Bible" booklets
Kevin Perrotta, *Genesis: God Makes a Start; Job: A Good Man Asks Why?; Psalms: An Invitation to Prayer; Jonah/Ruth: Love Crosses Boundaries; Mark: Getting to Know Jesus; Luke: The Good News of God's Mercy; Revelation: God's Gift of Hope; Acts: Good News of the Spirit*. Published by Loyola Press (see section D for address).

Little Rock Scripture Study program. Extensive printed, video, and audio materials, with leadership support services, for group Scripture study. Published by the Liturgical Press (see section D for address).

Periodicals
God's Word Today magazine. Explores the Bible book by book and by themes; for daily personal study, reflection, and prayer (see section D for address).

The Word Among Us magazine. Follows the lectionary readings day by day; for meditation and prayer (see section D for address).

8. Other materials
Saint Augustine, *On Christian Doctrine*, D.W. Robertson, Jr., trans. (Upper Saddle River, N.J.: Prentice Hall, 1958).

Raymond E. Brown, S.S., *Responses to 101 Questions on the Bible* (New York: Paulist Press, 1990); *Reading the Gospels with the Church* (New York: Paulist Press, 1996).

George T. Montague, S.M., *Understanding the Bible: A Basic Introduction to Biblical Interpretation* (New York: Paulist Press, 1997).

Peter M.J. Stravinskas, *The Catholic Church and the Bible* (San Francisco: Ignatius Press, 1996).

Periodicals
Scripture from Scratch. Video materials and newsletter, published by St. Anthony Messenger Press (see section D for address).

The Bible Today. Background and explanatory material about the Bible, published by Liturgical Press (see section D for address).

D. Publishers' addresses

Catholic University of America Press
P.O. Box 4852 Hampden Station
Baltimore, MD 21211
(410) 516-6953
www.cuapress.cua.edu

God's Word Today
P.O. Box 56915
Boulder, CO 80323-6915
www.GodsWordToday.com

The Liturgical Press
St. John's Abbey
P.O. Box 7500
Collegeville, MN 56321
(800) 858-5450
www.litpress.org

Loyola Press
3441 N. Ashland Ave.
Chicago, IL 60657
(800) 621-1008
www.loyolapress.com

Paulist Press
997 MacArthur Blvd.
Mahwah, NJ 07430
(800) 218-1903
www.paulistpress.com

St. Anthony Messenger Press
1615 Republic St.
Cincinnati, Ohio 45210
(800) 488-0488
www.AmericanCatholic.org

St. Vladimir's Seminary Press
575 Scarsdale Road
Crestwood, NY 10707
(914) 961-2203
www.svots.edu/svs-press

The Word Among Us
9639 Doctor Perry Road, #126N
Ijamsville, MD 21754
(800) 775-9673
www.wau.org

Index
Subjects, authors, works

Scriptural references